THE ERIE CANAL

MILESTONES
IN
AMERICAN HISTORY

MILESTONES
IN
AMERICAN HISTORY

THE ERIE CANAL

Linking the Great Lakes

TIM MCNEESE

CHELSEA HOUSE
PUBLISHERS

An imprint of Infobase Publishing

The Erie Canal

Copyright © 2009 by Infobase Publishing

Chelsea House
An imprint of Infobase Publishing
132 West 31st Street
New York, NY 10001

Library of Congress Cataloging-in-Publication Data

McNeese, Tim.
  The Erie Canal : linking the Great Lakes / Tim McNeese.
     p. cm. — (Milestones in American history)
  Includes bibliographical references and index.
  ISBN 978-1-60413-026-3 (hardcover)
  1. Erie Canal (N.Y.) 2. Erie Canal (N.Y.)—History. I. Title. II.
Series
  HE396.E6M36 2009
  386'.4809747—dc22   2008030743

Chelsea House books are available at special discounts when purchased in bulk quantities for businesses, associations, institutions, or sales promotions. Please call our Special Sales Department in New York at (212) 967-8800 or (800) 322-8755.

You can find Chelsea House on the World Wide Web at http://www.chelseahouse.com

Series design by Erik Lindstrom
Cover design by Ben Peterson

Printed in the United States of America
NMSG Bang 10 9 8 7 6 5 4 3 2 1

This book is printed on acid-free paper.

All links and Web addresses were checked and verified to be correct at the time of publication. Because of the dynamic nature of the Web, some addresses and links may have changed since publication and may no longer be valid.

CONTENTS

Guest of the Nation

He came to America as the first "Nation's Guest."[1] President James Monroe issued the invitation on behalf of Congress to the man whom many Americans considered the most famous Frenchman alive—the Marquis de Lafayette. The year was 1824. During the American Revolution, beginning in 1777, the aristocratic Lafayette had served as a volunteer aide to General George Washington. Lafayette was still in Washington's service in 1781 when the Americans and their French allies defeated the British in the last big battle of the war, at Yorktown, Virginia. When Lafayette first came to America, he was a young man of 20. Now he was 67 years old and in poor health, but he was determined to see America one more time.

As depicted in this painting, French military leader Marquis de Lafayette, who aided the American colonies in their fight for independence during the American Revolutionary War, received a hero's welcome. From August 1824 to September 1825, he would visit all 24 American states, covering 6,000 miles, including the nearly completed Erie Canal.

A HERO'S TOUR

Lafayette was treated to a whirlwind tour of the country he had helped to establish through revolution and war. For 13 months, beginning in August 1824, Lafayette visited all 24 American states. Congress gave him $200,000 and a grant of American land. His itinerary included stops at Harvard and Columbia universities. He attended formal dinners with "all three living ex-presidents, the current president, and the next president, and sat through what must have amounted to hundreds of speeches, dinners, toasts, and other forms of celebration."[2] Every city tried to outdo the others in its welcome to Lafayette.

In Boston, he rode in a carriage pulled by six white horses in a parade with 7,000 other participants. Some of the paraders were survivors of the 1775 Battle of Bunker Hill.

In the early summer of 1825, in New York State, the elderly Marquis was given an opportunity to see the latest technological creation of the young republic—the nearly completed Erie Canal. The canal was a wonder in the making. It stretched across the state from Buffalo to Albany, a distance of more than 350 miles. No other canal like it existed anywhere in the world. Tens of thousands of laborers had toiled in its construction. The work had included not only digging a 40-foot-wide, 4-foot-deep ditch, but also lining the waterway with stones and sealing it to make the canal as watertight as possible.

The canal was built over rugged terrain in upstate New York. The slope of the land fell more than 550 feet at more than one place along the east-west canal route. The building of the canal had required extraordinary feats of engineering and much architectural innovation. Where a river's path crossed that of the canal, engineers had ordered bridges and aqueducts built to convey the canal above the natural waterway. Where a gorge or other chasm interrupted the canal's course, workers had constructed an embankment to fill in the gap. And then there were the locks—83 in all, each a wonder of design. On the western section of the canal, at the new community of Lockport, engineers had designed a series of five locks built like stairsteps to carry the canal over the Niagara Escarpment, a huge rock ridge that otherwise would have blocked the canal's path. The locks had to be cut out of solid rock. In the summer of 1825, the slow and intricate work of creating the canal was soon to be completed. The Marquis de Lafayette could not help but be impressed at this latest creation of American ingenuity.

Lafayette began his tour at the canal's western end. He arrived in Buffalo, New York, on June 6, having traveled there by steamship. In 1817, when construction of the canal began, the first successful steamboat in America was only 10 years old. Lafayette took a carriage from Buffalo to Lockport. Along the way, he noted with wonder the great locks and aqueducts of the canal's elaborate system. He then boarded a canal passenger boat—called a packet boat—that carried him along the western canal route to such thriving towns as Rochester, Syracuse, and Utica. Beginning in Utica, Lafayette's host was the man who had made more contributions to the planning and construction of the canal than any other person in America: New York governor DeWitt Clinton.

CLINTON'S CANAL

Clinton's support of the canal project had come about as naturally as his lifelong support of the young American republic and his native state of New York. Clinton was born in 1769. As a young man, he became a lawyer and served as secretary to his uncle George Clinton, who was governor of New York. DeWitt Clinton also served in the New York State legislature and the United States Senate. As mayor of New York City, he was instrumental in establishing the city's public school system. From 1803 to 1815, with a couple of interruptions, he served as governor of the state of New York. In 1812, he ran unsuccessfully for president of the United States. He encouraged the development of steam travel on the Hudson River and fought for prison reform. The project into which he poured his heart and soul for most of a generation, however, was the building of the great canal that now crossed his state.

DeWitt Clinton was present at the groundbreaking for the canal in 1817. With a new shovel, he lifted the first scoop of soil—a scoop that would be followed by millions more during the eight long years of canal construction. As the canal neared completion, he still was on the scene. He ushered Lafayette onto a brand-new packet boat named for a great supporter of New York's great canal—the *Governor Clinton*.

The governor wanted to impress the marquis with his new canal. Not wanting to be outdone by Boston's carriage and six white horses, Clinton made arrangements for the marquis's boat to be pulled along the canal by a team of white horses instead of the usual mules. For three days, the governor and the marquis floated along the canal, sharing the leisurely experience. As they reached Albany, the state capital and the end of their journey, their boat floated beneath "a triumphal arch topped with a large stuffed eagle that flapped its wings by some form of mechanism at the moment of their arrival."[3] The canal trip was a highlight of the Marquis de Lafayette's last trip to America.

Lafayette sailed for his homeland just a month before the official ceremonies that marked the completion of the Erie Canal. The marquis had been wined and dined during his 13-month stay in America. He had experienced endless parades, ceremonies, dinners, and toasts in celebration of the American Revolution and American independence. Now, however, he would miss the celebration that might well have topped them all.

In October 1825, the $7 million construction project that in 1817 many people had believed could never be brought to completion was finished. The fanfare was spectacular. New Yorkers held jubilant celebrations of self-congratulation. New York State had built the canal alone, with no financial contributions from either the federal government or any other state in the Union, even though other states certainly would profit from the canal's existence. New Yorkers had fought with one another, argued about the merits of a canal across their state, and fussed about the cost of the project. They had mocked Governor Clinton for his hearty support of the project's potential and had dubbed the canal "Clinton's Folly." In the end, however, New York had rolled up its sleeves, hired the right engineers, surveyors, planners, and canal workers by the thousands, and produced a wondrous waterway unlike any other in the world.

How did it all happen? Who risked his career to see to the building of a canal across New York State? How was the rugged landscape of upstate New York tamed to allow a flat ribbon of water to flow across the state from Buffalo to Albany? Did the canal become a financial success? Did it play a major part in the destiny of the United States? The answers to some of these questions are found in the story of the canal's planning and construction. As New Yorkers celebrated in the fall of 1825, however, the answers to some of the others still lay in the future.

Transportation in Early America

From the founding of the first successful English settlement in North America at Jamestown, Virginia, in 1607 to the opening shots of the American Revolutionary War more than 160 years later, the colonists who lived along North America's Atlantic coast could not imagine moving far from the ocean. To the colonists, the lands that extended to the west were a mystery that loomed large in their imaginations. To move inland even 100 or 150 miles seemed to many to be a fool's errand. The interior meant separation from civilization. It meant living on the edge, uncertain of survival. It meant exposure to the possible hostilities of "wild Indians" who might well resent the intrusion of outsiders on their lands. The colonists may have been the descendants of intrepid souls who chose to leave England, Ireland, Scotland, and other European nations to make new homes in America. But the colonists saw no reason to move even farther from the few connections they still had with European civilization.

A MOUNTAIN BARRIER

During the first century and a half of English colonization in North America, there was another reason, too, why only a relative handful of people made the decision to pack up and move westward into such frontier territories as Ohio, Kentucky, and Tennessee. There was a mountain chain standing in their way. The Appalachians are not particularly high, but to the would-be pioneer or frontiersman of 1650, 1700, or even 1750, they represented a natural impediment to westward movement. The Appalachians actually are a series of elevated linear ridges— elongated strings of peaks that parallel one another, with few breaks in the chain to allow people to pass through easily. Because the Appalachian range extends from Maine in the north to today's Alabama in the south, the mountains worked against emigration into the backcountry to the west. Emigrants could pass with relative ease at only two natural breaks in the mountain chain. One, in western Virginia, is called the Cumberland Gap. This pass gave pioneers access to eastern Kentucky. The other break was located along the Mohawk Valley of upstate central New York. Thousands of pioneers did pass through the Cumberland Gap to Kentucky between the 1760s and the 1780s, but this flow of humanity was, in fact, no more than a trickle.

Another significant discouragement for Americans moving west during much of the colonial period was a lack of transportation routes into the interior. Roads in the colonies themselves were few and far between. Nearly all the land between the Appalachians and the Atlantic coast was forestland. Each acre was covered with hundreds of trees that ranged from maples to oaks to chestnuts. Many of the trees measured as much as 10 or 15 feet in circumference. A squirrel might be able to jump from tree to tree and reach its destination without ever touching the

The Cumberland Gap (*above*) was the chief passageway through the central Appalachian Mountains and was an important part of the Wilderness Road. The gap was used by American Indians and migrating animal herds. The path was widened by a group of loggers led by Daniel Boone, making it possible for pioneers to travel into the western frontiers of Kentucky and Tennessee.

ground, but the forests were an impediment to humans. Before roads could be built, trees had to be removed—a process that involved a considerable amount of human labor. The roads that did exist typically were nothing more than stretches of hard-packed earth. They became muddy and rutted with wagon and carriage tracks during rainy seasons. Travelers on such roads breathed in clouds of dust when the weather was fair and risked getting stuck in the mud when conditions were foul.

Although there were almost no substantial roads into the interior, there were trails. These were paths cut by American Indians. Some, perhaps, had seen hundreds of years of repeated use. These trails typically were quite narrow—certainly too narrow to accommodate wagons—but they did run toward the Appalachians and beyond, into the Ohio River Valley to the west. During the 1600s, approximately 300,000 American Indians lived between the Atlantic Ocean and the Mississippi River, more than 1,000 miles to the west. For centuries, Indians had traveled by foot all over their lands, often following buffalo trails. Over time, Indians developed trails of their own. These paths often were no wider than 12 to 18 inches across. Warriors following such paths often moved in single file, and generations of moccasins wore ruts a foot deep along these routes.

Several Indian trails were used by European colonists as they moved into the American interior. In the south, the Warriors' Path ran from North Carolina to Ohio. To the north, the Kittanning Path ran from eastern Pennsylvania across the Appalachians through Kittanning Gorge. Beyond the mountains, this path reached the Allegheny River, which became the headwaters of the Ohio River. Farther to the north, the Iroquois Trail ran westward from the Hudson River. The trail ran alongside the Mohawk River to Lake Erie, across modern-day New York. It is along this basic route that the Erie Canal one day would be constructed.

A FIGHT FOR THE OHIO COUNTRY

By the second half of the 1600s, colonists who lived in the Tidewater region of Virginia had developed a New World society mature enough to expand into the lands to the west, away from the Atlantic coast. Intrepid settlers began to move into the uplands of the Piedmont and the Great Valley of the Appalachians. The Piedmont is a plateau that lies directly east of the Appalachians. As early as 1671, colonial explorers from Virginia penetrated the region. They moved along the Blue Ridge, the easternmost hill line of the Appalachians. Small numbers of colonists settled in the Piedmont plateau and in the backcountry of Virginia and the Carolinas.

The clock was running down on the potential to colonize new lands east of the Appalachians, however. By 1725, most of the choice locations for settlement east of the Appalachians had been grabbed by the first explorers who moved west from the Atlantic coast. Throughout western Pennsylvania and the northern portion of western Virginia (modern-day West Virginia), little unclaimed land remained. New settlers and even some of the restless older ones moved south into southern Virginia and the Carolinas in search of new land for homes and farms. Eventually, sturdier pioneers pushed their way farther west, across the chains and ridges of the Appalachian Mountains. As the pioneers moved westward, a clash developed between the two dominant European powers in North America—Great Britain and France.

For generations, the French had occupied Canada. They had traded furs with American Indians and established scattered settlements of farmers, fur trappers, and powerful landowners. By the 1750s, the French were busy building a series of forts along the eastern Great Lakes. They located these forts directly in the paths of English colonial immigrants. The more forts the French built, the more the English in the 13 colonies decided that they were not willing to sit by and watch this part of the frontier be closed to them. In 1755, this conflict over what was known as the Ohio Country developed into a full-scale war.

At first, the war went badly for the British. By 1758, however, the British managed to turn the war around. This was thanks to a recommitment to the New World conflict by a newly appointed British prime minister named William Pitt. In the summer of 1758, the British captured a series of French forts, including Louisburg, on the coast of Cape Breton Island. In 1759, the strategic French site of Quebec fell to the British; Montreal was in British hands by 1760. Having triumphed in the war, the British extracted a harsh treaty from the French. The Treaty of Paris in 1763 ceded all of French Canada to the British and ended the European rivalry over the Ohio Country.

The end of the war did not lead directly to an official opening of the Ohio Country west of the Appalachians to English settlement, however. In an effort to limit potential clashes between the Indians living in the Ohio Country and English settlers, the British government issued the Royal Proclamation of 1763. This proclamation established the lands west of the Appalachians as an "Indian Reserve," a region that was to be set aside for occupation by the American Indians who had called the land home for hundreds of years. As of 1763, the mountain chain and a lack of wagon-worthy trails heading west no longer were the only obstacles that prohibited the movement of American colonists into the interior. British policy now did the same thing, at least officially. Despite the policy, some Americans still ventured into the Ohio Country, into Kentucky, and enterprising businessmen formed land companies after 1763 to sell western land to American pioneers.

ANOTHER CONFLICT

By the next decade, the British and their American subjects were at war with each other. A revolutionary spirit swept through the colonies, and angry colonists protested British policies that increased taxation and furthered British controls. The American Revolution delivered extraordinary change to the people of the 13 colonies who fought a war against their mother country. The 13 colonies became 13 states and banded together to form the United States of America as they declared their independence from Great Britain. The fighting dragged on for six-and-a-half years, until 1781. It stopped when British general Charles Cornwallis surrendered to American general George Washington at the sleepy little tobacco port of Yorktown, Virginia. Two years later, in 1783, both nations signed the Treaty of Paris, which concluded the war and marked a new beginning for the young American nation. The United States of America emerged from the war larger than it had been when the 13 former colonies entered the conflict. Under the treaty, the United States was given land from the Atlantic Ocean westward to the Mississippi River and from the Great Lakes southward to Spanish Florida.

Gone were the British officials, and gone was the Proclamation of 1763 that officially had closed the frontier to colonial migration. Now the United States government would determine future policies regarding the western frontier. Many Americans, especially those already living in the trans-Appalachian region, were excited about their future prospects. Despite the Proclamation of 1763 and the Revolutionary War itself, western migration had never ceased. After an entire generation of western movement, even such remote places as Kentucky and Tennessee were home to thousands. By 1785, the non-Indian population of Kentucky, which technically was part of Virginia until it became a state in 1792, had grown to more than 30,000. By the end of the 1790s, the settler population of Kentucky had increased by an additional 45,000. To the south, in Tennessee, 36,000 immigrants had established their frontier homes by 1800. Immigration also was picking up for the Ohio Country north of the Ohio River.

In this painting, British military commander Charles Cornwallis and his troops surrender to George Washington and French commander Comte de Rochambeau in Yorktown, Virginia. The Siege of Yorktown was the last major land battle of the American Revolutionary War, as the surrender of Cornwallis's forces prompted the British government to negotiate an end to the war.

Despite the success of the American Revolution, the new nation still faced problems that involved European powers. Even though they had agreed to do so under the Treaty of Paris, the British did not immediately abandon their western forts, which were strung out along the Great Lakes. More than once during the years that followed the end of the Revolutionary War, Spain would not agree to American dominance east of the Mississippi River. Spain blocked American access to this great interior trade route and effectively cut off the port of New Orleans from American commerce. Despite these obstacles, many Americans believed that the key to the future growth of the United States lay in the lands of the trans-Appalachian

West. Congress gave the region much attention as it tried to secure the rights, privileges, and loyalty of the independently minded pioneers who already lived there and those who wished to follow them.

Two treaties became central to the government's policy of protecting the trans-Appalachian frontier. In 1794, President George Washington dispatched Supreme Court Chief Justice John Jay to London to negotiate a treaty that, among other provisions, drew yet another promise from the British to evacuate their forts along the American side of the Great Lakes. This time, the British did as they promised. The following year, Washington sent a fellow southerner, Thomas Pinckney of South Carolina, as an envoy to Spain to negotiate an agreement by which Spain opened up the Mississippi River to American trade. Pinckney's Treaty—known to the Spanish as the Treaty of San Lorenzo—gave Americans the right to ship their goods along the Mississippi and to export them, without paying a duty, out of the port of New Orleans. The treaty gave a significant benefit to westerners in search of markets for their agricultural produce. All Americans continued to keep their eyes on the trans-Appalachian West.

The 1790s saw increasing numbers of American settlers and their families pouring into the trans-Appalachian region. A government road—Zane's Trace—was authorized from western Virginia into Ohio. The Lancaster Pike into western Pennsylvania was built and opened by 1797. By 1800, the number of pioneers living in the West between the Appalachians and the Mississippi River had reached 500,000. In 1790, 95 percent of America's population lived in the Atlantic seaboard states. By 1820, one out of every four Americans lived west of the Appalachians.

WESTERN MOVEMENT AFTER THE WAR

As the new republic grew, a conflict developed between Great Britain and the United States. England had a heavy-handed practice of stopping American merchant ships bound for France, a country with which Great Britain was at war. The British seized cargoes and even kidnapped American sailors. In 1812, the United States and Great Britain were at war themselves. The War of 1812 ended in a stalemate in 1815, but the years that followed the war offered new hope to the United States and its western territories.

Prior to the war, Great Britain had worked against American emigration into the trans-Appalachian region by holding on to its Great Lakes forts and supporting American Indians in the western backcountry of the territory known as the Old Northwest. These actions and other factors may have caused the number of emigrants to remain artificially low and slowed the speed of western movement. By 1815, more than 500,000 Americans had settled on lands in Kentucky, Tennessee, and Ohio and in western Pennsylvania and New York. These settlers were scattered across a vast region that extended from the interior valley of Canada's St. Lawrence River to the southern reach of the Tennessee River. Despite 40 years of American migration over the Appalachians into western lands from Tennessee to Kentucky to Ohio, by the end of the War of 1812, "more than two-thirds of the new nation's population still lived within 50 miles of the Atlantic seaboard, and the center of population rested within 18 miles of Baltimore."[1]

In 1815, the western regions still were little more than frontier outposts. Western towns such as Buffalo and Rochester, New York, had not yet been founded. Cincinnati, on the Ohio River, was home to 15,000 people; this was because of the importance of that river as a waterway to carry pioneers westward. One of the greatest restrictions to American emigration west of the Appalachians was, in fact, a lack of transportation routes into the West. By 1815, there were only two roads to convey people on horseback across the Allegheny Mountains. American Indians lived and traveled across the Old Northwest as far west as modern-day Illinois. These Indians included the nations of the

Kickapoo, the Miami, the Wyandot, and the Shawnee. In the Old Southwest, Indian tribes such as the Cherokee, the Chickasaw, the Choctaw, and the Creek called the modern-day states of Alabama, Mississippi, Georgia, and Kentucky their home. As for new states emerging from the trans-Appalachian West, none were added during the decade between Ohio's entry into the Union in 1803 and the opening of the War of 1812. Even someone as astute and intelligent as former president Thomas Jefferson believed, in 1803, that it might take Americans as long as 1,000 years to fill in the lands between the Appalachians and the Mississippi.

Jefferson may have been among those who were surprised when the number of Americans moving west of the Appalachians after the War of 1812 signaled the start of a great wave of emigration. Pioneers poured into the Old Northwest's Ohio, Indiana, and Illinois. South of the Ohio River, other intrepid settlers rushed into northern Georgia, western North Carolina, Alabama, Mississippi, Louisiana, and Tennessee. Within seven years, five new western states were added to the growing Union: Louisiana (1812); Indiana (1816); Mississippi (1817); Illinois (1818); and Alabama (1819). From the banks of Indiana's Wabash River to the lower reaches of the Mississippi Valley, Americans were on the move.

As they moved westward, the settlers wanted to replicate the lives they had known back east as quickly as possible. Many had moved west in search of cheap land. To this end, the U.S. government was happy to cooperate. In the early nineteenth century, the federal government's income was derived largely from two sources: trade duties and land sales. The government owned so much land that land was looked on almost as an inexhaustible natural resource. Beginning in the mid-1780s with the passage of the Ordinance of 1785, and continuing with a similar act in 1796, the federal government sold western land in squares of 640 acres, with each block of land measuring one square mile. These ordinances restricted the government from

After the American Revolution, Congress implemented the Land Ordinance of 1785. This grant brought a new system of measuring and distributing land that had been acquired from Great Britain north and west of the Ohio River. For the first time, farmers were able to claim sole ownership of the land and were assured of clear boundaries and firm titles.

selling small divisions of land, however, and at a price of $1 an acre under the Ordinance of 1785, many Americans could not afford a square mile of property. When the 1796 act raised the minimum per acre to $2, it raised the price for 640 acres of western land to an even more out-of-reach $1,280. The two acts further retarded the sale of western land by not allowing people to buy on credit. Sales were on a cash basis only.

In 1800, a third federal act remedied these roadblocks to westward advancement. Through the Land Act of 1800, the federal government began selling its western properties in tracts that measured 320 acres and allowed the land to be purchased on credit. Suddenly, western land was not only available, but also within the price range of more potential buyers. By 1820, Congress made it even easier for would-be pioneers to buy

ORGANIZING THE NORTHWEST TERRITORY

Starting in the 1780s, the U.S. government passed a series of ordinances to support and encourage American emigration to the lands west of the Appalachian Mountains and to help organize the western territories as quickly and efficiently as possible. In relatively short order, Congress passed a pair of laws related to the West, and especially to the area known as the Northwest Territory. With the Mississippi River serving as the western border of the young United States, the lands west of the Appalachians and east of the Mississippi were viewed as two great regions. The dividing line between these regions was, essentially, the Ohio River, which flowed from east to west until it reached the Mississippi. The region that became known as the Old Southwest included the modern-day states of Kentucky (the Ohio River basically formed Kentucky's northern border), Tennessee, Mississippi, and Alabama. The Old Northwest, bordered on its south by the Ohio River, included the modern-day states of Ohio, Indiana, Illinois, Wisconsin, and Michigan.

To organize the Northwest Territory, Congress first passed the Land Ordinance of 1785. This act authorized a survey of the region and set up a mechanism for the sale of western surveyed lands. The Northwest Ordinance of 1787 established an initial system of government for the Old Northwest. The act allowed the eventual creation of no more than five and no fewer than three states to be carved out of the region. The act also recognized the rights of Americans living in the territory, making those rights identical to the rights enjoyed by citizens in the original 13 states. The law also established a process by which a territory eventually could become a state.

land. The government began to sell land in even smaller parcels, some as small as 80 acres. The government also dropped the price per acre to $1.25. The would-be pioneer of 1796 paid $1,280 in cash for 640 acres. The ambitious frontier family of 1820 paid $100 for 80 acres and did so on credit.

Even as these adventurous Americans moved farther west, however, they did not want to sever ties with the eastern states that they had left behind. The emigrants wanted to maintain connections with the East, and especially trade connections. They viewed access to eastern markets as a key to their frontier survival. To get their western produce—bales of cotton, herds of pigs, bushels of corn, and jugs of whiskey—to eastern markets, they needed better transportation systems. The men and women of the West wanted new roads and canals not only to facilitate their movement west, but also to help keep them connected with buyers back east. Following the War of 1812, the U.S. Congress responded by authorizing construction of a national road to cross the Appalachians into Ohio and continue on to points farther west. In various states of the Union, there was talk of building other roads and canals. No state took the prospect of a westward canal more seriously than did the state of New York.

Early Canal Pioneers

Modern historians have little doubt about the identity of the first European to reach the region of modern-day upstate New York. His name is forever linked to the region's history and geography: Henry Hudson. Hudson first reached the wilderness of today's New York on September 10, 1609, when he sailed his ship, the *Half Moon*, into what is now New York Harbor. Hudson was an Englishman, but the Dutch had hired him to explore North America in search of an all-water route to the Far East: the elusive, legendary Northwest Passage. Hudson was not the first European sea captain to reach the waters of New York Harbor, however. That honor goes to an Italian mariner named Giovanni da Verrazzano (his last name is often spelled *Verrazano* today), who arrived in 1525. Hudson explored farther up the river that someday would bear his name than any explorer before him, however. On that September day, he saw a broad

In this painting, Henry Hudson is greeted by American Indians on the shores of the Delaware Bay. Seeking a Northwest Passage, Hudson and his crew sailed around the Chesapeake and Delaware bays in August 1609. He then moved into New York Harbor and proceeded up what is today the Hudson River, making it as far as Albany before realizing that it was not the Northwest Passage.

river mouth that might lead him exactly where he wanted to go. He continued past what today is Manhattan Island and headed up the Hudson.

During the following nine days, Hudson sailed the *Half Moon* 150 miles up the river, all the way to today's Albany, New York. He encountered many curious American Indians along the route. North of the Albany site, he reached a river that entered the Hudson from the west. Because it was narrower than the Hudson, it did not appear to be the route to the Far East. This river was the Mohawk, which one day would parallel much of the route of the Erie Canal.

Hudson continued up his one-day namesake river for several more days. He encountered more Indians, and he and his crew got drunk on a concoction the Indians called "hooch-enoo," a word that would give rise in the future to a slang word for alcohol: *hooch*. Eventually, Hudson turned back. The Hudson River became increasingly shallow, no more than seven feet deep, so he had little choice but to sail south. He left the region altogether and sailed back to Europe, having failed in his quest for the Northwest Passage. Hudson did not see the potential of the land or of the narrow river that he scorned—the Mohawk.

A GLOWING REPORT

One of the first Europeans to take a serious look at the landscape of central New York did so in the early eighteenth century. He looked at the land with an eye to tapping its potential for economic development and fully utilizing its unique water systems. His name was Cadwallader Colden. Colden was an Irish-born Scottish immigrant. In 1724, the captain general and governor of provincial New York, William Burnet, named Colden as his surveyor general. Burnet could not have chosen a better man for the job. Colden was a multitalented individual. He was a medical doctor, a scientist, and, of course, a surveyor. Even before his immigration to America, he was recognized as a scientist. He published papers in mathematics, botany, medicine, philosophy, and natural history. These works were well regarded by Colden's colleagues. One of his works was read aloud by the great British astronomer Edmund Halley before the Royal Society of London for the Improvement of Natural Knowledge, an important scientific organization.

Colden was described as "tall, with a round face and a protruding nose."[1] In later life, he became lieutenant governor of New York, but he found himself out of step with the growing revolutionary spirit of the era. When New Yorkers wanted him to take a stand against the British parliament's move to place a Stamp Act on the American colonies, he refused. Throughout the

American Revolution, Colden remained loyal to King George III. Yet this stubbornly loyal British subject had a crucial and positive impact on American history.

In 1724, Governor Burnet dispatched Colden into the western reaches of the colony of New York. Colden's orders were to report back on the region's natural topography and the presence of the French, who were extending their influence south from Canada, across the St. Lawrence River. During his trek into western New York, Colden became keenly aware of the significance of the geopolitical struggle that was going on between the British and the French in the North American interior. He wrote about the Iroquois Indians who were caught up in the struggle of the two European colonizers. He wrote about the history of the New York province, including the continuous clashes between English and French colonists. He also wrote about the region's longtime contribution to the fur trade—a trade largely controlled by the French that he believed the English could cut in on. (The title of his report to Burnet was "A Memorial Concerning the Furr-Trade of the Province of New York.") These aspects of his report reflected a study of cultures, history, and international politics.

The report that Colden delivered to Governor Burnet was concerned primarily with the region's geography, topography, and climate, and with its various waterways—lakes as well as rivers. The report ran to an impressive 6,000 words. It was a rich and descriptive document. Colden devoted considerable length to a description of the differences between Canada's St. Lawrence River and the lakes and rivers that ran across New York, especially between the Hudson River and Lake Erie in the west. These bodies of water, argued Colden, would provide the English with "the key to an easy victory over the French."[2]

Colden described the St. Lawrence, the only major river in French Canada that provided its colonists with access to the Atlantic Ocean, as a river subject to "tempestuous weather and thick fogs . . . the navigation there is very dangerous. . . . A voyage to Canada is justly esteemed much more dangerous than to any other part of America."[3] Those who navigated the St. Lawrence struggled on a river with tides that crested to 20 feet and currents that were so strong that boats regularly capsized or were splintered on the rocks along the shores. Colden insisted that travel on the St. Lawrence by night was quite impossible.

On the other hand, Colden described the rivers of the English colonies in positive terms. He considered them more navigable and tame. He offered high praise to the Hudson River, describing it as far superior in every way to the St. Lawrence. The Hudson, wrote Colden, is "very straight all the way [into northern New York and the mouth of the Mohawk], and bold, and very free from sand banks, as well as rocks; so that the vessels always sail as well by night as by day, and have the advantage of the tide upwards as well as downwards."[4] With only 150 miles separating New York City from Albany, the Hudson placed an ocean port within easy reach of upstate New Yorkers.

Colden also reminded the governor that a mere 110 miles of easy-rolling New York countryside separated the Hudson from the province's other important upland river, the Mohawk. Here, Colden wrote, the central New York mountains "seem to die away as they approach the Mohawk River."[5] On reaching the Mohawk, an imaginary traveler from New York City had already covered 40 percent of the distance from the great seaport to Lake Erie, which lay approximately 230 miles due west, with largely flat countryside in between. (The actual elevation difference between the headwaters of the Mohawk River and Lake Erie is only about 100 feet.) To Colden, it was the Mohawk that would serve as the foundation for a navigation system across the colony. He described how smooth

The Mohawk Valley was a land of strategic importance. For more than 10,000 years, American Indians lived in this river corridor, followed by European and American settlers. During the French and Indian War, many battles were fought here between the British and the French (and Great Britain's Indian allies, the Iroquois). In 1825, the Erie Canal was completed off the Mohawk River tributary, linking the Hudson River and Port of New York with the Great Lakes.

the river was, and how gentle, with a fall of approximately one foot for every mile over its first 40 miles. A traveler then would reach Little Falls, where the stream dropped a sudden 40 feet. Below the falls, the river followed another 62 miles of slow drop in elevation, approximately 2 feet per mile. It was at the river's end that the traveler would encounter his greatest difficulties, "where the river drops more than two hundred feet over sixteen miles between Schenectady and the point where it empties into the Hudson, just north of Albany."[6] Still, claimed Colden, taking the Mohawk as a whole, including its precipitous waterfalls, the river dropped only about four feet per mile.

Beyond the Mohawk River, to the west, that same imaginary traveler could continue on to Lake Erie by canoe, following a relatively straight line along a series of smaller streams separated by short distances easily covered by carrying the canoe from water to water. With such a simple "water route" across New York, Colden was certain that the English could make a place for themselves in the lucrative fur trade. After all, he argued, "in every thing [such as] diligence, industry, and enduring fatigues, the English have much the advantage of the French."[7]

LITTLE PROGRESS

Despite Colden's positive descriptions of the New York waterways and the way they would facilitate travel from one end of the colony to the distant other, New Yorkers did not follow up on many of the surveyor's suggestions about involving themselves in the western fur trade. Nor did New York's colonial leaders try to develop a systematic transportation route by water across the colony. More than 40 years passed before another New York voice, that of Governor Sir Henry Moore, suggested in 1768 to the legislature, "The improvement of our inland navigation is a matter of the greatest importance to the province, and worthy of their serious consideration."[8] Even then, little was done. The British had established a trading post at Oswego in 1727, three years after Colden submitted his report, to facilitate trade with the Indians. During the next two years, the English constructed a large fort. The trading post proved extremely popular.

During the following half century, New York experienced great change as the underlying conflict between the English and the French erupted into a full-scale clash of arms. The French and Indian War of the 1750s and 1760s was soon followed by the upheaval of the American Revolution. By the early 1780s, Americans had gained control of their political destinies. Great Britain had lost the Revolutionary War, and the former colonists were eager to get on with establishing their new nation—the United States of America. Many eyes looked to the West, to new lands. The territory of western New York was still considered a frontier, and the region began to see new development. Although nearly two centuries had passed since the arrival of the first Europeans in the New York region, much of the Mohawk Valley still remained as unaltered as it ever had been. The region between the Hudson River and Lake Erie was primeval, a land "of dark forests, roaring waterfalls, and meandering streams."[9] It would fall to a later generation of New Yorkers to deliver great changes to the unspoiled landscape.

A CANAL DREAMER FROM VIRGINIA

In the survey report that Cadwallader Colden wrote in the early 1700s, he expressed his belief that the Mohawk Valley of central New York might provide a viable route into the West. The New York legislature was located right in the middle of the vast watery corridor, at Albany. Between 1784 and 1817, the year construction began on the Erie Canal, that legislature dithered back and forth on the issue of enhancing a water route, but to no avail.

No one followed up on Colden's vision of an augmented waterway into the western frontier until the years after the American Revolutionary War. The man who did so was not a New Yorker, but a Virginian. Like Colden, he was trained as a surveyor. He was a man of wealth, a solid administrator, a natural-born leader, and a man with "a keen eye for real estate."[10] He was, by the 1780s, the most famous of Americans: George Washington.

(continues on page 32)

During the late 1700s, the 13 states, which were located along the Atlantic Coast, feared that other nations would be able to claim the interior of North America. George Washington proposed building a canal that would unite frontier America with the settled states. Although Washington's Patowmack Company failed, citizens of New York took up his plan to build a canal that would reach hundreds of miles westward.

George Washington emerged from the Revolutionary War as the general who had led the Continental Army to victory. In the 1780s, he returned to his dream of establishing a company to build a canal system on the upper reaches of the Potomac River, a vision he first had fostered during the early 1770s. A year after the end of the war, Washington set out on horseback into western Virginia. His purpose was to plan, "as much as in me lay, the inland navigation of the Potomac."* His secondary purpose was to view land that he owned in the region—thousands of acres that had been granted to him by the British government for his services in the French and Indian War of the 1750s and 1760s.

Washington returned from his investigations of the upper Potomac more convinced than ever that a canal system could be built. He wrote to the governor of Virginia to suggest that a company be established to order the specific survey work necessary for a water project that might connect the Potomac River with the Ohio River beyond the Appalachians. This company would become the Patowmack Company.

Washington worked closely with the new company. He raised money through the sale of company stock at a price of 50 pounds per share. In all, the company was financed with 250 shares of stock that sold for a total of 12,500 pounds, an amount equal to approximately $1,125,000 today.

To construct the canal, Washington tapped James Rumsey, a mechanically minded innkeeper whom Washington met during his trip west in 1784. Rumsey intrigued Washington with a model of a boat that he said could travel up rivers. He demonstrated his invention "in a large shallow pan through which water could flow rapidly."** Rumsey had never worked on a canal, but he so impressed Washington that the general offered him the job. "I have imbibed a very favorable opinion of your mechanical ability," Washington wrote to the

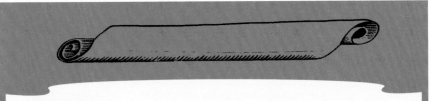

Virginia innkeeper, "and have no reason to distrust your fitness in other respects."*** Rumsey signed an agreement on July 14, 1785.

Things did not go well with Rumsey on the job, however. At every turn, the unique work of building the canal presented problems. Laborers had to work in frigid waters as the Potomac cascaded out of the mountains. Some workers turned to alcohol, especially rum, to warm themselves, and this frustrated Rumsey: "Every time they get a little Drunk, I am cursed and abused." [†] Rumsey was responsible for approximately 1,000 workers in all. Discouraged by low wages, many of the original workers had to be replaced by slaves and Irish laborers. Rumsey himself seemed to spend more time trying to apply steam power to his model rivercraft than he did working on the canal. The canal company's directors fired him in July 1786.

Despite these setbacks, work on the canal moved ahead. By 1788, Washington was no longer directly involved as president of the canal company because he had been elected president of the United States. The locks on the Little Falls of the Potomac were completed by 1795, nine years after Rumsey left the project. The work on the Great Falls locks continued for seven more years. By the time those locks were completed, George Washington, the dreamer of the western canal, was dead.

Washington never lost sight of his vision of a western canal. He rose from his sickbed just four days before his death on December 14, 1799, to write out instructions to his representative, a man who was commissioned to vote Washington's 77 shares of canal company stock at an upcoming meeting.

* Peter L. Bernstein, Wedding of the Waters: The Erie Canal and the Making of a Great Nation. *New York: W.W. Norton, 2005, 66.*
** *Ibid, 68.*
***Ibid, 73.*
†Ibid.

(continued from page 28)

Washington was one of the earliest advocates of developing a waterway into the vast western interior of North America. Prior to the Revolutionary War, Washington watched as his fellow colonists began to cross over the Appalachian Mountains in limited numbers. He began to fear that if an easy water route was not created to serve as a connection between those who lived east of the mountains and those who crossed over them, a natural, psychological divide would grow that would add to the natural distance. This would result in a trans-Appalachian country separate from the original 13 colonies.

To prevent the growth of this divide, by the early 1770s, Washington began to develop plans for a man-made waterway based on the Potomac River to link the west with the east. He believed that a series of short canals could be constructed to bypass a couple of waterfalls on the upper Potomac and so allow navigation farther west on the river. By 1772, Virginia officials gave him permission to establish a Potomac navigation company. Washington's plans were soon interrupted, however, by the outbreak of the Revolutionary War. Throughout the conflict, as he led American troops, Washington never forgot his dream of a Potomac canal system.

After the war, Washington returned to his canal campaign. He received a go-ahead in 1785 from both the Virginia and Maryland legislatures to charter the Patowmack (the original spelling of the word *Potomac*) Company. Work began on the canal the following year. It involved hundreds of workmen, including immigrants and slaves. At the Potomac's Great Falls, five locks were built to bypass the 77-foot drop in the river. The work at the falls was not completed until 1802—three years following Washington's death—but parts of the Patowmack Canal were in operation by 1788. "Washington's Canal" was in service for 40 years. During that time, it delivered $10 million worth of goods to market. By 1830, however, the canal company went bankrupt. Washington had pioneered across western Virginia what Colden had suggested for New York—a water route into the West.

New Canal Voices

By the 1780s, George Washington's vision of a western canal was on its way to becoming a reality. At the same time, dreamers elsewhere in America were contemplating the possibilities of western canal projects in their own states, including New York. Cadwallader Colden's report was 60 years old, but the time had come for serious-minded men of a new generation to look closely at the prospects of building a canal within the borders of New York State. One of these men was another of America's Founding Fathers, a patriot named Gouverneur Morris. As early as 1777, during the Revolutionary War, the wealthy Morris was advocating improvements along the Mohawk River to allow for easier navigation. Morris envisioned a water route that would deliver boats from the Hudson River to Lake Erie. Throughout the war, he maintained his optimistic view that such improvements could be made in the

Mohawk Valley. In the years after the war, he would "cease to be just a rooter for the canal and would assume an active role in its development."[1] His most important contribution would come a decade after the war's end.

AN IRISH WATER MAN

Another canal advocate of this era was an Irish veteran of the Revolutionary War, a man whom DeWitt Clinton once described as "a man of good character, an ingenious mechanician, and well skilled in mathematics."[2] His name was Christopher Colles.

In November 1784, Colles appeared before the New York State legislature with an idea for a western water route across the state. It is unclear why he became interested in a canal project centered on the Mohawk River. There is no evidence that he had read Colden's 1724 report. But there he stood, addressing the legislators about altering the Mohawk River "so that boats of burthen [burden] may pass the same."[3] For the New York lawmakers, Colles was a man to listen to on this subject.

Before coming to America, Colles worked on water projects along Ireland's River Shannon. During the 1770s, he designed a water-delivery system for New York City—an engineering marvel in its day. It was a system of pipes made from hollowed logs that transported water from the city's reservoir (located under today's Criminal Courts Building) to another reservoir situated at the southern end of Manhattan Island. In the fall of 1784, this expert in water projects caused the state legislators to prick up their ears.

When Colles addressed the legislature a second time, in May 1785, he convinced the lawmakers to pay him $125 (approximately $2,250 in modern dollars) to work up a full-blown building plan for a waterway along the Mohawk River to the river's headwaters along Lake Ontario. By 1786, the New York legislature granted Colles the right to establish a company to improve navigation across the state. The innovative Irishman failed to draw enough support from would-be investors, however, and his ideas lost their steam. He soon abandoned the project altogether. Despite this setback, Colles did not give up entirely on his desire to have an impact on America's transportation systems. During the next several years, he worked to create the first detailed road map of the United States.

NEW VOICES FOR CANALS

Colden, Morris, and Colles each played a singular role in the decades-long campaign to convince a skeptical public that a canal route across central New York represented the best future not only for the region but for the western movement of American pioneers. It would remain for yet another man of vision to produce the first real efforts to alter navigation in New York. He was a dreamer with a memorable name—Elkanah Watson.

Watson was born in 1758. As a young man, he worked as an apprentice to a wealthy merchant. During the Revolutionary War, he served as a courier between military commanders and on more than one occasion delivered messages to Benjamin Franklin in Paris. His service to the revolutionary United States government gave him opportunities to meet many important people, both in America and Europe. These people included not only Franklin, but also Founding Fathers John Adams, Alexander Hamilton, and Aaron Burr; American painters John Singleton Copley and Benjamin West; British statesman Edmund Burke; and Scottish scientist James Watt. On one visit to London, during a night at the opera, Watson was introduced to the Prince of Wales, the man who later became England's King George IV.

Throughout his life, Watson was a tireless traveler. Prior to the Revolution, he toured the American colonies from New England to Georgia. He also traveled widely in Europe, to England, France, Italy, and Holland, usually in the company of important people. Watson wrote in detail about his tours.

In 1791, Elkanah Watson and a group of prominent New Yorkers surveyed the state for potential settlement opportunities. Watson, who had
a great interest in canals, proposed a small, man-made waterway for
the area to increase trade and transportation opportunities. This idea
for a small canal was later expanded to run from Lake Erie to the Hudson River.

On nearly every trip, he took special notice of canals. He was charmed by the man-made waterways of the Low Countries. Canals became a lifelong source of fascination and study for him, and he put that fascination to practical use in America. In 1785, Watson met with George Washington at his Mount Vernon estate. Washington told Watson of his plan for a canal on the Potomac. When Watson showed great interest in the project, Washington encouraged him to come live along the Potomac and be a part of the plan. Watson declined. He already had an interest in pushing for the construction of a canal system that included the Hudson River. Watson had traveled along both the Potomac and the Hudson, and he declared that the New York river was the only other in America that compared to the Potomac "in magnificence and utility."[4] Washington and Watson talked of canals for two days, and the conversation encouraged Watson's interest in man-made waterways. He later wrote that his visit with Washington "completely infected me with the canal mania and enkindled all my enthusiasm."[5]

It was a mania on which Watson acted. In 1788, the canal supporter made a business trip to western Massachusetts. While in the region, he decided to take a side excursion to Albany, the New York capital, and then proceed up the Mohawk River. Several things soon impressed him. He found the upstate scenery enthralling; in his writings, he described the mountains, the abundant farm fields, and "the rich fragancy [sic] of the air, redolent with the perfume of clover."[6] He also noticed the number of emigrants passing through the region on their way west. Watson made note of the lack of good roads, the number of bridges in disrepair, and the lack of decent inns for lodging and public houses in which one could find a good meal. By the time Watson reached the headwaters of the Mohawk River, he already was convinced of the need of a canal. As he later wrote, "a canal communication will be opened, sooner or later, between the great lakes and the Hudson."[7] All his life, Elkanah

Watson claimed that he was not only the first person to encourage the laying of a new navigation system across central New York, but also the first to imagine the Erie Canal.

Having passed along the Mohawk Valley yet again, Elkanah Watson returned from his trip more convinced than ever that a canal system could and should be constructed and that such a system would provide untold economic change to the New York region. One excited canal enthusiast was not sufficient to convince enough of the right people that such a project should be undertaken or that it would be successful. Through the remainder of the 1780s, Watson collected information and courted supporters. In the fall of 1791, he brought his supporters together and led them on a trip out of Albany along the Mohawk Valley. He gave them an opportunity to see the future for themselves.

During the tour, the group traveled along half the length of the future Erie Canal. They passed through a region with more wild animals than humans. They did not visit a western New York town with a population larger than a few thousand. They admired the rich farmlands of the region, but they saw that the farms were scattered, with "just a tenth of the eight million acres of land along the future route of the canal . . . under cultivation."[8] In short, Watson's party saw a land rich in resources waiting to be tapped.

The group returned to Albany impressed with what they had seen. They became true converts to their host's dream of a canal across the Mohawk Valley. They also imagined that they might profit from the substantial tolls that such a canal could generate.

It must be noted that even Watson was not imagining a canal of the scope of the one that was built across New York in the early decades of the nineteenth century. He created plans to build a canal only from Albany to Utica, New York, a distance equal to approximately one-third the length of the Erie Canal to come. In fact, in later years, when the actual canal was being built, this self-proclaimed first dreamer of a central New York canal admitted that he had never imagined such an elaborate project. In his words, "we never entertained the most distant conception of a canal from Lake Erie to the Hudson. We should not have considered it much more extravagant to have suggested the possibility of a canal to the moon."[9]

AN IMPORTANT MEETING

After returning from his trip with his supporters, Watson met with influential New York State senator Philip Schuyler. A former general, Schuyler had fought across upstate New York during the Revolutionary War. It did not take a conversation with Watson to convince Schuyler to support a canal. He already was a supporter, having visited England before the war, during that country's great canal boom period. Schuyler's support was important to Watson. Schuyler was a powerful politician, a war hero, and the father-in-law of Alexander Hamilton. Founding Father Hamilton was now United States Secretary of the Treasury. Schuyler told Watson that he would give his support to a canal project and gave Watson instructions to draw up a plan to accompany possible legislation. In a report to the state legislature later that year, Watson emphasized the economic vitality such a canal would offer New York. Watson claimed that even a short canal, one that only connected the headwaters of the Mohawk to nearby Wood Creek, would allow New York to "open a water communication from the Atlantic that would be the most extensive in the world."[10]

Was Watson's claim based on wishful thinking, or on reality? Could the Mohawk River be altered for better navigation? Could a new navigation system or canal translate into a financial boon for New York State? The answers were both yes and no. On one hand, Watson probably overstated how easily the Mohawk could be tamed for navigation. In 1804, Timothy Dwight, the president of Yale University, noted that the

Philip Schuyler, a lifelong New Yorker who grew up in Albany, believed in Watson's proposed canal plan. With Schuyler's support and influence, Watson was successfully able to present his idea to the state legislature.

Mohawk was "so imperfect merchants often choose to transport their commodities along its banks in wagons."[11] With such questions concerning a canal connecting with the Mohawk River, the decision was made to construct a water route that was completely man-made.

On the other hand, Watson's claim that an improved waterway across the state would bring economic benefits probably was understated. Prior to the building of the Erie Canal, goods were moved across the state by wagon rather than by water because there was no complete waterway. To span the distance between Albany and Schenectady required the building of 27 canal locks to deal with the region's steep hills. There were approximately 50 sets of rapids in the 62 miles of the Mohawk River between Schenectady and Little Falls. The 40 miles from Little Falls to Rome, New York, included an additional 22 rapids. Such geography held back the economy of central New York. Getting goods to market was laborious and expensive. In the end, however, Watson's words were convincing. By early spring in 1792, the New York legislature passed the Mohawk Improvement Bill. A spate of additional bills followed and were passed in rapid succession. These bills created the Western Inland Lock Navigation Company, the purpose of which was to develop a water route along the Mohawk to Lake Ontario, or even, if feasible, to the Finger Lakes to the west. A second company—the Northern Inland Lock Navigation Company—was authorized to create a navigable water route north from the Hudson to Lake Champlain. Philip Schuyler was selected as president of both companies, and Elkanah Watson was included on the Western Company's board of directors.

Even as the two companies set out to accomplish their goals, the building of a true canal was not considered the first order of business. Locks might be constructed, as the names of both companies inferred, but only to bypass existing rapids and falls. This was the way Washington's Patowmack Company had been built. Nothing in the bills that led to the establishment of the two companies hinted at a complete canal system that would bypass local rivers.

EARLY CONSTRUCTION

Despite the promising start-ups of the companies, everything did not proceed according to plan. Because the two inland lock navigation companies were established as stock companies, the purchase of shares provided the capital for construction. Each company was authorized to sell 1,000 shares at $25 per share. As an incentive to investors, stock purchases could be paid for over time rather than all at once. The initial purchasers included "merchants, businessmen, and bankers from New York."[12] Sales were slow, however, and 15 of the first 36 individuals to buy shares owned lands adjacent to the Western Company's suggested route. In May 1792, Schuyler tried to boost stock sales by increasing the number of his own shares in the Western Company from 10 to 100. In the end, however, only 743 shares out of 1,000 were sold, and one-third were surrendered when company officials asked for more money to provide needed capital. The owners of one-third of the shares purchased in the Western Company gave up their shares rather than invest more money when the request was made to increase the amount of investment made by these shareholders. Most stock owners never saw much profit from their investments.

Some construction did take place, but setbacks became common. Eventually, 400 workers were employed on the navigation projects. Many of the workers were Irishmen. Proposed locks between Albany and Schenectady were meant to allow boats to bypass Cohoes Falls. The work proved too complicated for the engineers on hand, however. (Even 30 years later, when the Erie Canal was constructed, this stretch would prove to be a tough nut to crack.) At Little Falls, engineers had better success. They built five locks along a mile-long stretch of the Mohawk. Each of these locks was designed to raise boats up nine feet. Farther west, a pair of locks was built near Rome, New York. These locks created a connection between the Mohawk River and Wood Creek—a connection that cut the time needed to pass through the region by water from a day to an hour. These early locks were constructed out of wood. This construction proved impractical, however, as the wood in the locks soon rotted out and the locks began to leak profusely. In 1803, many of the wooden locks were replaced with locks built of brick and stone, yet these, too, leaked. What was needed was a durable mortar that could withstand constant contact with water. As these few projects were completed, the Western Company was able to point to increased traffic along the Mohawk. Yet the tolls that were collected were never enough to provide a profit for investors and cover maintenance costs. Schuyler resigned from the Western Company, having been elected to the U.S. Senate in 1789. The man whose Senate seat he took was DeWitt Clinton.

All was not failure for the Western Inland Lock Navigation Company, however. The improvements that were built made navigation on the Mohawk more practicable. Workers not only constructed locks, but also cleared sandbars, rocks, and sunken trees from the river and built several small dams to increase the Mohawk's summer water flow. The locks may have been less than efficient, but they did allow travelers to pass around Little Falls, and they also shortened the distance of travel by linking the Mohawk with Wood Creek. The backbreaking work of portaging—carrying boats overland around the river—was eliminated.

Ultimately, the work of the Western Inland Lock Navigation Company was a failure. Watson always hoped that the company could achieve greater success than it did. The failure of the company rested in the amount of money that the company had to work with: Western Inland always was underfunded. Great work was accomplished, however. The company "was in many ways a proving ground and training school for the great artificial waterway that would one day span the state all the way

DURHAM BOATS: THE RIVER'S WORKHORSES

As the progressive and talented dreamers and engineers of the Western Inland Lock Navigation Company retooled basic navigation on the Mohawk River, those who sailed along the river entered a new era. Previously, boatmen on the Mohawk had relied on simple boats called bateaux that were easy to portage but small: Each bateau was limited to carrying fewer than two tons of goods. With the improved navigation provided by the lock system, portaging was largely eliminated. The building of the locks allowed boatmen to begin using another type of cargo-carrying vessel—a flat-bottomed model called a Durham boat. It would become the new workhorse of the Mohawk.

The Durham boat was named after an engineer from Pennsylvania named Robert Durham. Durham built these river vessels back east in about 1757. These boats were first used in great numbers on the Delaware River. In 1776, Durham boats carried American troops under George Washington's command across the Delaware to surprise the enemy at Trenton with a Christmas Day attack.

Durham boats were larger than bateaux. A Durham boat measured about 65 feet in length and 8 feet across the beam—the widest part of the boat. It was flat-bottomed. The crew propelled a Durham boat with 18-foot-long oars. Durham boats could carry much more weight than the smaller bateaux—as much as "twenty tons of iron or 150 barrels of flour on their downstream runs."* A Durham boat had a single 30-foot mast on which a sail or sails could be rigged. This allowed the boats to move forward faster, even in slow water. Durham boats required a seven-man crew, including the captain. A Durham boat traveling upstream relied on four men at the oars and another two who pushed against the current with poles.

(continues)

(continued)

Following the engineering improvements of the Western Company, Durham boats covered the distance between Schenectady and Lake Oneida without leaving the water. Because a Durham boat had a capacity 10 times greater than that of a bateau, the Durhams helped Mohawk River boatmen to increase their profit margins even as they reduced the amounts they charged for their services. This resulted in a great increase in traffic along the Mohawk. According to the Western Company's report for 1798, the improvements on the river and the use of Durham boats had brought about a drop in the cost of hauling goods between Albany and Geneva from $100 per ton to $32 per ton. On the river route between Albany and Niagara Falls—the entire distance, east to west, across New York State—freight rates were cut by 50 percent.

It is interesting to compare these cuts in transportation costs to freight-wagon costs in the region. Generally, to make a suitable profit, merchants and producers had to keep transportation costs—the costs of getting their goods to market—down to no more than half of the price that was charged to the consumer. Freight-wagon rates were so high between Buffalo in the west and Albany in the east, however, that transportation costs sometimes were five or six times higher than the value of the goods themselves. Suddenly, improvements along the Mohawk and the use of Durham boats changed that equation dramatically.

*Bernstein, 98.

from the Hudson to Lake Erie."[13] In little more than a decade, the Western Company made over the Mohawk River Valley and altered the Mohawk River into a deep-water route that could accommodate heavy-duty Durham boats along a significant portion of the future length of the Erie Canal. Another valuable contribution is also clear: A significant number of the engineers and politicians who one day helped to bring the Erie Canal into being were first involved with the Western Company. What held back the Western was, quite simply, money. Future water projects, including the Erie Canal, would achieve success only when alternate types of financing, including state funding on a grand scale, became the norm. By the early nineteenth century, that day was not far away.

New Plans for an Artificial River

Because of the improvements to navigation on the Mohawk River made by the Western Inland Company, the idea of carving anything like a full-scale canal across central New York was not considered seriously at the dawn of the new century. Then, in 1803, the New York State surveyor general, Simeon DeWitt (cousin to DeWitt Clinton, the future "Father of the Erie Canal"), had a conversation with his friend Gouverneur Morris. Morris had supported improved navigation along the Mohawk Valley since the late 1770s. He suggested to the surveyor general the possibility of "tapping Lake Erie . . . and leading its waters in an artificial river, directly across the country to the Hudson River."[1] DeWitt, who was familiar with Morris's canal dreamings, considered the suggestion "a romantic thing, and characteristic of the man."[2] An assistant to DeWitt, James Geddes, seconded his boss's opinion. Geddes considered Morris's idea to be highly impractical.

A FLOUR MERCHANT NAMED HAWLEY

Two years later, however, someone else made the same suggestion to Geddes in a conversation during dinner. Geddes had a boarder in his home in Geneva, New York. The boarder was a flour merchant from the Finger Lakes region named Jesse Hawley. Hawley had become convinced that a canal across the state was just what merchants needed.

The region's roads were still in miserable condition, nearly unfit for hauling freight by wagon. The roads were little more than old Indian paths, dusty in summer and muddy in winter and spring. During their dinner conversation, Hawley told Geddes of his belief in the need for an upstate canal. After the meal, Hawley and Geddes looked over a map of New York, and Hawley pointed to Lake Erie. He stated that the water required for such a canal would come from that large inland body. Hawley was neither an engineer nor a surveyor. He did, however, believe that a canal was possible.

During the next few years, Hawley's belief in a canal across central New York remained a theory. The canal-dreaming merchant continued to use the improved navigation provided by the Western Inland Company in his work as a flour dealer, even as the tolls charged were so high that he could not make a profit. By 1807, Hawley found himself serving a 20-month sentence in debtor's prison in the Finger Lakes–region town of Canandaigua. During his months in prison, Hawley wrote a series of 14 essays in which he not only favored building an inland canal system, but also outlined the system on paper. He wrote the essays under the pen name Hercules. Hawley described how Lake Erie could be utilized to provide water for the man-made system and stated that such a system would bring new prosperity to upstate New York. The first of Hawley's essays was finished within his first three months in prison and

In the early days of the United States, transportation methods were inefficient and expensive. Like the future frontiersmen traveling to the West, merchants had to use covered wagons to transport their goods to their customers. The Erie Canal would provide a faster, cheaper alternative that would increase trade and improve the economy of New York State.

was published in the *Genesee Messenger*, a local newspaper. The last of his essays was published in April 1808.

Specifically, Hawley argued in support of a canal running east to west across the state. The route was a natural one, one established by "the Author of nature," said Hawley.[3] In one essay, Hawley wrote of the lengths to which God already had gone in preparation for a possible canal across central New York:

The Creator has done what we can reasonably ask of him. By the Falls of Niagara he has given a head to the waters of Lake Erie sufficient to flow into the Atlantic by the channels of the Mohawk and the Hudson, as well as by that of the St. Lawrence. He has only left the finishing stroke to be applied by the hand of art, and it is complete! Who can reasonably complain? . . . If the project be but a feasible one, no situation on the globe offers such extensive and numerous advantages to inland navigation by a canal, as this![4]

Hawley described the basic route that he thought was most feasible for a canal and wrote at length, in striking detail, about the different construction techniques to be utilized. His "interior route" would create one long canal running from the Hudson River to Lake Erie. Other canal dreamers supported another route, the "lake route." That route would include a canal from Albany to Lake Ontario, with boats continuing on to the Niagara River, an overland portage around Niagara Falls, and then on to Lake Erie. Although the lake route allowed a shorter canal, it also placed the route closer to British Canada. In 1807, the United States and Great Britain were engaged in trade conflicts and other hostilities that were tilting the young republic toward war with its former mother country.

Hawley's plans for an "artificial river"[5] drew the immediate attention of New York's legislators. By 1810, in a joint resolution, the New York State legislature took its first significant step toward eventual construction of the Erie Canal. The legislature appointed a seven-man commission to take charge of building a canal across New York. All of the commissioners were wealthy, and all were New Yorkers. They were Gouverneur Morris, Stephen Van Rensselaer, DeWitt Clinton, Simeon DeWitt, William North, Thomas Eddy, and Peter B. Porter. It was a well-chosen commission of canal supporters, each of whom represented a particular political constituency, including the two main political parties of the day, the Federalists and the Democratic Republicans. Although they were inspired, in part, by Hawley's essays, the New York legislators also had another incentive for considering the construction of a canal across their state. They thought that they might receive some financial support from the United States government.

JEFFERSON AND GALLATIN

In 1804, United States president Thomas Jefferson was reelected to a second term. On March 4, 1805, in his second inaugural address, the president proudly told the American people that his administration was presiding over a federal government with an expanding budget surplus. He even spoke of completely retiring the national debt in less than a decade. Jefferson also proposed ways that those surplus federal dollars might be spent. He suggested that "the revenue thus liberated may, by a just repartition of [the surplus] among the States . . . be applied in time of peace to rivers, canals, roads, arts, manufactures, education, and other great objects within each State."[6] In the immediate years that followed, Jefferson's claims of federal government surpluses continued to ring true. In 1806, the surpluses ran ahead of his estimates. In early 1807, Jefferson spoke again of surplus monies being spent on "internal improvements."[7] His words might have been intended specifically for the ears of the legislators of New York State, who already were considering a canal of their own.

The United States Senate was controlled by the Republican Party (Jefferson's political party, founded as the Democratic-Republicans). The Senate backed the president's calls for federal support of major transportation projects. On March 2, 1807, the Senate authorized Albert Gallatin, the secretary of the treasury, to draw up "a plan for the application of such means as are within the power of Congress, to the purposes of opening roads, and making canals . . . which as objects of public improvement, may require and deserve the aid of government."[8] Gallatin soon drew up just such a report. He understood that transportation improvements such as roads and canals would have a dramatic impact on the nation's economy. Merchandise and other cargoes that passed easily and cheaply from one region to the markets of another region could only translate into an increase in America's wealth.

In his report, Secretary Gallatin actually mentioned the possibility of building a canal between the Hudson River and Lake Erie, a project to which he gave first-rate importance. In his specifics, Gallatin did not mirror Hawley's proposal for an interior route. Instead, he suggested two canals. One would follow the Mohawk River and then run up to Lake Ontario. The other would connect Lakes Ontario and Erie, using the Niagara River but bypassing the great falls. Gallatin even placed a price tag on this elaborate lake-route system: $3 million. That was less than half the amount it eventually would require to construct the Erie Canal.

NEW YORK LEGISLATORS TAKE STEPS

With Jefferson's words of encouragement, the New York legislature began to pursue its plans. On February 4, 1808, even before receiving word of Gallatin's report, a New York assemblyman from Onondaga County, Joshua Forman, introduced a resolution in the state legislature:

> Whereas, the President of the United States, by his message to Congress ... did recommend, that the surplus moneys in the treasury ... be appropriated to the great national objects of opening canals.... And whereas, the state of New-York, holding the first commercial rank in the United States, possesses within herself the best route of communication between the Atlantic and western waters ...[9]

Forman then proposed that a joint committee be established to examine, through a survey, the best possible route for a canal to connect the Hudson River with Lake Erie, with the hope that the U.S. Congress might provide monies for the project, just as President Jefferson had indicated. Forman was mocked by some legislators—by those uncertain of the president's promise or skeptical that such a canal was feasible—even as he presented his resolution. Despite the mockery, he continued making his proposal. In the end, the New York State legislature listened. In April 1808, the legislature agreed to spend $600 on a survey. The amount was small, but it marked another step.

With instructions to carry out a survey, State Surveyor General DeWitt handed off the job to his number-two man, James Geddes. Geddes was more interested in a possible canal route from the Hudson River to Lake Ontario, however. He did not favor the route Forman suggested, to Lake Erie. DeWitt told Geddes to focus on a canal to Lake Ontario and to do a quick survey on the other route. Through the summer of 1808, Geddes traveled around upstate New York. He studied the topography and the rivers along the Mohawk Valley. Because the survey was underfunded, Geddes even spent $73 out of his own pocket. As a canal advocate, he was willing to do so. The legislature later paid him back.

As he made his survey, Geddes also made an important discovery. Previously, it was believed that the region east of Rochester, near Palmyra, was not a good location for a portion of any canal because "the ground [was] situated so far above the level of the rivers and lakes that there would be no source of water to supply a canal."[10] Geddes found, however, that the Genesee River was situated high enough on both sides of the Irondequoit Valley that it could provide water to feed a canal that would allow boats to pass between the local hills. Fourteen years later, when the Erie Canal was nearly completed, Geddes wrote about this startling revelation: "I felt disposed to exclaim Eureka, on making this discovery. Boats to pass over these arid plains, and along the very tops of these high ridges, seemed then like idle tales to every one round me."[11]

Even as Geddes spent the summer of 1808 examining a possible canal route or routes across New York, Simeon DeWitt

Before building could begin on their new project, the state legislature commissioned a survey of the area to determine the best route for the Erie Canal. James Geddes determined which parts of New York's uneven landscape were viable for building, along with areas that would require additional construction. Many canals of that time needed inclines to allow boats to travel between different canal levels.

did not remain idle. If a canal were to be constructed to Lake Erie, questions might arise concerning access to land on which to build such a canal. The biggest question was centered on the region between the Genesee River and Lake Erie. Much of the region was owned by the Holland Land Company, a private firm that was owned by six Dutch banks. The company had been formed a decade earlier and was selling lots and farms to would-be settlers. Land sales were not booming, however. When DeWitt contacted the company's resident agent, Joseph Ellicott, the Holland Company representative proved to be enthusiastic about a canal. Roads in the region were poor; most were old Indian paths. A canal would draw a new wave of emigrants into western New York. Ellicott heartily endorsed the building of a canal across his company's property and even offered company money and land to help facilitate the canal's construction. Ellicott made it clear, however, that he favored only one canal, not two, and that the single canal should connect with Lake Erie. Ellicott also was a surveyor. He provided DeWitt with a detailed survey of the region and a map.

By late 1808, DeWitt had everything he needed to present President Jefferson with a solid plan for building a canal across New York State, financed, at least in part, with federal monies. DeWitt sent his plans to Washington City and heard nothing. With no response from the president, Joshua Forman—the legislator who had quoted Jefferson in his presentation to the New York legislature—went to Washington City in January 1809 to meet with the president.

Much had changed since Jefferson's inaugural address almost four years earlier. The Jefferson administration was on a collision course with Great Britain. The looming conflict concerned England's practice of harassing American merchant ships on the high seas, especially ships carrying cargoes to France. The English also were taking American sailors from American ships and impressing them into the British navy. In December 1807, Jefferson had pushed the latest in a series of trade restriction acts through Congress. This act had drastically reduced the international trade of the United States in an attempt to force the British to end their destructive practices against the young nation. The resulting trade embargo had caused stagnation in the U.S. economy. The surpluses of which Jefferson had spoken so proudly back in 1805 had disappeared.

Jefferson had spoken of the government's surpluses being spent "in time of peace [for] rivers, canals, [and] roads."[12] Now, however, peace was drifting away, and clouds of war were looming on the horizon. Jefferson was blunt with Forman. The president said, "You talk of making a canal of 350 miles through the wilderness—it is little short of madness to think of it at this

ROBERT FULTON
(1765–1815)

CANAL SUPPORTER

Albert Gallatin's 1807 report to Congress offered many examples of possible transportation projects, as well as facts and figures. The secretary of the treasury did not originate these details all on his own, however. He took some suggestions from an expert on water projects and a variety of other subjects—inventor (and fellow New Yorker) Robert Fulton.

Today, Fulton is remembered chiefly for inventing the first practical, commercially successful steamboat in America. There was much more to Robert Fulton than inventive steamboating, however. He was not only a mechanic *extraordinaire*, but also a man who, earlier in life, had made a living by painting miniature portraits. Before 1800, he invented a basic submarine and tried to sell it to both the British and the French. No one in either country had enough insight into the future to invest in Fulton's invention, however. Fulton was creative, self-promoting, and probably as smart as any man in America in his day. Fulton combined "many of the talents of P.T. Barnum, Thomas Edison, Bill Gates, and Leonardo da Vinci."* He also had studied canal building.

Fulton added detail to Gallatin's report by listing examples of places around the country where canals should be constructed. He knew that such man-made waterways would reduce freight-transportation costs and build up the nation's overall economy. He estimated the cost of building canals in America at $15,000 per mile. Even though construction of the Erie Canal did not begin for nearly another decade, Fulton's per-mile estimate came surprisingly close to the per-mile cost of that New York water project, the total cost of which was $6 million.

Gallatin's report included an example, supplied by Fulton, of an imaginary American canal system. Fulton's theoretical canal

(continues)

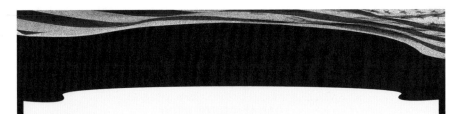

(continued)

boat would be worked by a man, a boy, and a horse. The boat would have the capacity to move 25 tons of freight a distance of 20 miles a day. Fulton estimated the cost of the man, the boy, and the horse at a total of $2.50 per day. He estimated the cost of maintaining the canal at $2 per day. He even added 50 cents per day to the cost for wear and tear to the theoretical canal boat. According to Fulton's estimates, it would cost $5 per day to provide a water system to transport 25 tons of cargo over a distance of 20 miles. That cost factors out to 20 cents per ton over the same distance, an amount equivalent to $1 per ton per mile. By comparison, Fulton figured, the cost of hauling the same amount of cargo by road, using horses and wagons, would cost 10 times that amount. Even with all his statistics, however, Fulton missed the true bottom line in his contribution to the Gallatin report: By cutting transportation costs from $10 per ton to $1 per ton, "it would be profitable to move a far greater variety and quantity of goods to market."**

   Even as he provided information for Gallatin's report to Congress on the feasibility of constructing a canal to connect the Hudson River and either Lake Erie or Lake Ontario, Fulton was busy on another project. Fulton had returned to the United States in the fall of 1806 after 20 years abroad. He spent the year after his return building his second steamboat, the *Clermont.* He demonstrated his boat successfully in August 1807, on the Hudson River. It was, of course, that same river that the Erie Canal later opened to the West.

---

*Bernstein, 115.
**Ibid, 117.

day."[13] Forman understood: There would be no federal money for a New York canal. Even as Forman left the president's company on that disappointing January day, however, he assured Jefferson that "the state of New-York would never rest until [the canal] was accomplished."[14]

DeWitt Clinton and Friends

Despite Forman's assurance to President Jefferson that New York would build a canal even without federal support, the possibilities seemed remote. Because the president had held out the possibility of using federal surpluses to fund such internal improvements, the New York State legislators had agreed only to fund a survey. Without federal support, would the state legislators be willing to gamble with state money? It seemed unlikely.

INTERNATIONAL EVENTS
Other events taking place beyond the borders of New York also were casting shadows over the future of an inland canal. Jefferson's Embargo Act had crushed the nation's trade economy. The act had closed all American ports to foreign shipping. In

fact, the act hurt the United States more than it did any other nation. All American ports were hit hard, but New York suffered the most. By spring 1808, activity along the piers and wharves of New York Harbor was almost nonexistent. As one English observer wrote, "The few solitary merchants, clerks, porters, and laborers that were to be seen were walking about with their hands in their pockets. The coffee-houses were almost empty; the streets, near the water-side, were almost deserted; the grass had begun to grow upon the wharfs."[1]

The embargo's impact rippled across the country. In western New York, the Holland Land Company saw its land sales plummet. Jefferson's embargo proved to be such an ineffective policy that Congress repealed it by March 1809 and replaced it with the Non-Intercourse Act. That act allowed American shippers to get back in business but still banned British and French imports to the United States. Conflict with Great Britain and France remained the order of the day. By 1812, the United States would be at war with Great Britain. The idea of a canal across New York still had its supporters, however. The seven-man commission was in place by 1810, and no one among the seven played a more important role in the future of a New York canal than DeWitt Clinton.

THE FATHER OF THE ERIE CANAL

DeWitt Clinton was born in 1769, in the Hudson River Valley, at Little Britain, near Newburgh. Even as an adolescent, he was in love with New York City, which lay 75 miles downriver. At age 15, he attended Columbia College; he graduated in 1786. In adulthood, Clinton was a constant servant to his native state. His first wife, Maria Franklin, was a beautiful woman who came from a wealthy family. The couple had 10 children, 9 of whom survived into adulthood. Clinton was a good and loving father. He took such an active role in his household that, despite his official duties, he did much of the family marketing.

Governor DeWitt Clinton worked tirelessly for New York, and served in various national and local political positions, including state assembly-man, U.S. senator, and mayor of New York City, before being elected governor. As an avid outdoorsman, he was heavily involved with the Erie Canal project.

Clinton had a keen interest in history and loved the outdoors. He was an amateur scientist of sorts; ornithology—the study of birds—was a lifelong fascination. Clinton was a man comfortable with the thought of leading others. He was "tall and broad, with a notably high forehead, clear eyes, and a set expression around the mouth. He was never someone to be trifled with, as his many enemies would learn to their sorrow."[2]

Clinton got his first taste of public service while working as secretary to his uncle, New York governor George Clinton, who held the office between 1777 and 1795. DeWitt Clinton was elected to the United States Senate and served for part of a term between 1802 and 1803. He was elected mayor of New York City three times and served a total of 10 years, from 1803 to 1807, from 1808 to 1810, and from 1811 to 1815. By the time Clinton was mayor, New York City was the nation's largest city and saw the greatest traffic in exports and imports through its magnificent harbor. As mayor, Clinton provided free public education to the city's poor children and established the city's first fire insurance company. He was known to follow city fire wagons to help put out fires. Mayor Clinton helped establish a free asylum for the insane that became part of Bellevue Hospital. In his later years, Clinton was elected twice as New York's governor. His first election was in 1817, while the Erie Canal was under construction. He was governor again when he died, in 1828. Few men held greater sway over the political direction of New York, both city and state, during the early nineteenth century than DeWitt Clinton.

As a member of the seven-man canal commission, DeWitt Clinton took his responsibilities seriously. By the spring of 1810, the New York State legislature had accepted a canal proposal made by Thomas Eddy, one of the first directors of the Western Inland Company, and his friend State Senator Jonas Platt. Eddy and Platt supported a canal across central New York, utilizing the waters of the Mohawk and Seneca rivers. Eddy and Platt were, in fact, the men who originally proposed the formation of a seven-man canal commission, a commission that included Eddy himself. Five of the commissioners recommended by Eddy and Platt were shareholders in the Western Inland Company. Eddy and Platt felt, however, that they had to have the unquestioning support of DeWitt Clinton. They recommended him for the commission. They felt they would not have a hard time convincing Clinton to support a canal. To seal his support and that of the other commissioners, however, Eddy and Platt organized a fact-finding expedition to travel across central New York to see how a canal could be built and where. The expedition involved five of the commissioners, including Clinton. Morris and Van Rensselaer did not travel the entire trip with their colleagues, but met up with them later in western New York.

A TRIP ALONG THE MOHAWK

Clinton and Eddy traveled together up the Hudson River in early July, on Robert Fulton's three-year-old *North River Steamboat*, the vessel that was later known as the *Clermont*. The full five-man group gathered at Albany and set out in a pair of bateaux that they named the *Eddy* and the *Morris*. The expedition was on its way across central New York. The commissioners traveled through lands that were still, to an extent, frontier. Some inns along the way were decent and offered good food. Others were dingy and dirty. As Clinton wrote in his journal, the travelers at times were "assailed by an army of bed-bugs, aided by a body of light infantry in the shape of fleas, and a regiment of mosquito cavalry."[3]

They passed through towns such as Utica and Rome. There they saw signs of progress and industry, including a Utica cheese factory and a cotton mill. The men noted that the varied scenery included rolling hills and great gorges. They knew that these would have to be conquered if a canal was to be built. DeWitt Clinton did some bird-watching; he caught sight of 23 different varieties. When the expedition finally reached Lake

Robert Fulton, a submarine designer, was brought to the United States to collaborate with businessman and ambassador Robert Livingston on a river steamboat. His first successful ship, the *Clermont*, shuttled people from New York City to Albany and also transported Governor DeWitt and his commissioners.

Erie, the men were welcomed aboard the only U.S. naval vessel on the lake, the *Adams*, a 150-ton brig armed with four cannons. The commander of the *Adams* told the commissioners that ships that sat seven feet into the water could sail across the lake to "Chaquagy [modern-day Chicago] and then up [the] creek of that name to the Illinois River . . . and so down to the Mississippi."[4] In these words, the commissioners all heard the same message: Their canal, if constructed, could unite the waters of the Atlantic, at New York City, with the waters of the Gulf of Mexico, thousands of miles to the south.

The commissioners' exploratory travels took almost two full months, after which they returned to write their report to the New York legislature. They knew the importance of the canal, and they knew that their report might make or break its future. Among their number, Gouverneur Morris was the loudest opponent to the canal project. One of the most vexing issues was the question of how to fund the massive project. The hope of federal aid was all but gone. Jefferson was no longer president; a fellow Virginian, James Madison, had been elected to replace him in 1808. The commissioners pushed for the canal to be constructed using public money, with ownership and control of the canal to be held by the state of New York. This was a singular step on the commissioners' part because critics of a canal, including those in the state legislature, thought it could not be built without "the revenue of all of the kingdoms of the earth, and the population to China, to accomplish it."[5] The commissioners also agreed that any canal to be built must be a completely man-made waterway and stretch more than 300 miles from the Hudson to Lake Erie. The commissioners took six months to commit their findings to paper. They finished their report in March 1811. Clinton took the lead in preparing legislation to be presented to the state's lawmakers.

As soon as the commissioners made their report public, the critics made their voices heard. Others applauded the commission's efforts. What mattered most, however, was that the report soon led to the presentation of a canal bill before the state legislature, and that the bill managed to pass. The canal bill earmarked $15,000 to be made available to the commission for future work. It also gave the commission permission to buy out the old Western Inland Company and arrange financing for a new canal project. The commission also was empowered to begin negotiating for land purchases along the route. Eddy and Robert Fulton were sent out to find the right engineers for the project. Morris and Clinton were tapped to go down to Washington City to see whether any money at all was available.

The planets seemed to be lining up in favor of a long, long canal across New York, from eastern river to western lake.

The way to a canal did not go smoothly, however. The three years that followed the commission's presentation to the state legislature were, in fact, exceedingly bumpy. Despite the fact that the commission included Federalists, some Federalist politicians claimed that the canal was nothing more than a Republican-backed scheme. It appeared to Morris and Clinton at first that President Madison would give his support, but the president soon began to claim that the Constitution might not allow federal money to be spent on a state canal project. Although Gallatin was still secretary of the treasury, he was no help. Neither was Congress.

THE THREAT OF WAR

The commissioners continued with their plans, even as the threat of war with Great Britain continued to mount. In 1812, they presented a second report to the New York State legislature, in which they pointed to the threat of war as a reason for a canal. As Clinton argued, "The prospect of war made the canal project all the more imperative."[6] The 1812 report also included the estimated cost of a canal: $6 million. In view of the fact that there now were more than one million inhabitants of New York State, that amount did not seem staggering to many. The commissioners also estimated the increased economic activity that the canal would likely create. They predicted that, within 20 years of its completion, the canal would carry 250,000 tons of freight each year. A toll of $2.50 per ton on freight going in both directions along the canal would produce annual income for the waterway of $1.25 million. Even if the amount of freight were to fall to half that estimate, the commissioners noted that it would still generate $600,000 in revenue annually. That would be enough to pay interest of 6 percent on the construction project even if the canal were to cost tens of millions of dollars. The commissioners clearly envisioned the canal as "a key to the commerce of our western world."[7] In June 1812,

STEAMING UP THE HUDSON

In the summer of 1810, the New York Canal Commission hit on yet another way of pushing along the possibility of a canal across their state. They decided to travel to upstate New York and travel around to examine areas through which a canal might run. Five commissioners traveled out to Albany together, toward the Mohawk River. They did not all reach Albany by the same mode of travel, however. Two of the commissioners traveled up the Hudson River in relative style, on the most cutting-edge means of inland water travel in the United States: America's only steamboat.

DeWitt Clinton and Thomas Eddy sailed as passengers on Robert Fulton's *North River Steamboat* from New York to Albany. Fulton's boat was the first of its kind. A side-wheel paddle steamer, it measured 149 feet in length, 18 feet from side to side at it widest point, and weighed 182 tons. At the boat's center was an elongated cabin with a ceiling height of six feet, six inches, "sufficient for a man with a hat on," according to Fulton.* Early steamboats such as Fulton's often were described as unattractive vessels, as seen in the following report written by an English traveler to America in 1830: "[They are] the least picturesque [of vessels]. . . . Their smoking chimneys . . . their ungraceful and worse than dromedary projections, give the idea of a floating foundry."** Such steam-powered craft were not popular for their appearance. They were appreciated for what they could do that no other rivercraft of their day could do: travel upriver in a straight line at a pace of four or five miles per hour.

The fare on Fulton's steamboat was not cheap. It was equal to $1 per 20 miles of river, or $7 for the 150-mile trip between New York City and Albany. (When the Erie Canal was built a few years

the legislature approved the commissioners' borrowing of $5 million to continue making surveys and laying further groundwork for a canal.

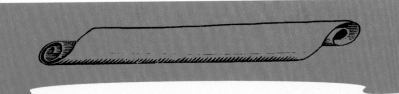

later, the fare on the canal between Utica and Rochester, a distance of 152 miles, was about the same.) For their money, passengers on Fulton's steamboat were treated well. If, from the outside, the boat looked utilitarian, it was far from spartan in its accommodations. Fulton decorated his steamboat with touches that included "ornamental paintings, gilding, and polished woods."*** The cabin section included 54 rooms for passengers, space for cooking meals, and a bar. Meals were not included in the price of a ticket. Lunch was served at 2:00 P.M., and an evening meal was available at 8:00 P.M. Each meal cost 50 cents. If they wished, passengers could eat on deck, under an awning that protected them from sun or rain.

In an attempt to attract socially upscale passengers, Fulton established rules for those who took passage on his steamboat. Because sleeping rooms were assigned on a first-come, first-served basis, early-boarding passengers had their pick. Fulton fined anyone who reclined on his bed with his boots on. Smoking was allowed only below decks and was restricted to men. Card players were required to stop playing at 10:00 P.M. so that they would not keep other passengers awake.

Clinton and Eddy spent 40 hours on the *North River Steamboat* on their voyage from New York to Albany. Although Clinton kept a journal of his trip with the canal committee, he wrote little about his voyage on Fulton's steamboat. The boat arrived in Albany just after sunrise on Monday, July 2, 1810.

* Bernstein, 143.
**Ibid.
***Ibid.

By summer 1812, however, most plans for the canal ceased for all practical purposes. The threatened war between the United States and Great Britain had finally erupted following a June address to Congress by President Madison for a declaration of war against Great Britain. Canal commissioner Stephen Van Rensselaer was appointed head of the New York militia. In the fall, DeWitt Clinton ran as a peace candidate for U.S. president. He lost, even though he was supported by both Federalists and Republicans who were unhappy with President Madison. By 1815, at war's end, Clinton was no longer mayor of New York City.

Some steps were taken to keep the canal project alive. A bill to buy out the Western Inland Company passed the New York legislature in 1812, on the day after Madison asked for a declaration of war from Congress. The commissioners hired an engineer; ironically, he was an Englishman. In their 1814 report, the canal commissioners suggested that the canal be augmented by another water project to Pennsylvania's Susquehanna River Valley to the south. The Holland Company donated more than 100,000 acres of western land to clear the path for a canal. As the war continued, however, the future of the canal looked dim. By 1815, the whole project seemed on the verge of collapse. As Joseph Ellicott of the Holland Land Company wrote to a friend, "The Canal bubble it appears has at length exploded."[8]

All was not lost, however. So much time, effort, ingenuity, legal study, real estate dealing, and engineer dreaming had gone into the planning of a canal across New York State that the War of 1812 only managed to postpone the inevitable. The war ended officially, in December 1814. (The Battle of New Orleans was fought in January 1815, three weeks after the signing, in Europe, of the treaty that ended the conflict.) New Yorkers waited only two more years before every element was finally in place for the construction of a canal. Much of the credit for putting those elements in place goes to DeWitt Clinton and his fellow commissioners, who never completely abandoned the project during the first half of the 1810s. Even at the low point of 1814, "the commissioners had launched a program which would be carried by its own momentum and the force of circumstance."[9] The canal would be built, even in the wake of a war.

Construction on the Canal Begins

One important factor that affected the timing of building a canal was the War of 1812. Significant campaigns were fought in upstate New York, and "military embarrassments on the Niagara frontier were attributed in part to the bad roads between Washington and Buffalo."[1] The cost of delivering military goods and hardware into western New York during the war was prohibitive. When some cannon were dispatched from the nation's capital to Buffalo, New York, the cost of shipping the cannon was five times more than the value of the artillery itself. After the war, with the British still in control of Canada, the United States needed to build up its presence in the Great Lakes region. Furthermore, as people began to move westward through the region in greater numbers than before the war, the need for a canal became even more crucial.

THE COMMISSION TAKES ACTION

The commissioners acted in 1815. They invited 100 likely financial supporters of a canal to meet at New York City's City Hotel on December 31. At the same time, Dewitt Clinton spearheaded a subcommittee to convince the state legislature to take up the issue of a canal as soon as possible. Legislators were shown detailed plans for a canal that included 62 locks to deliver boats up and down a total of 625 vertical feet along the canal's length. (In earlier years, there had been discussions about the use of an inclined-plane system, rather than a system of locks, to pull and lower boats up and down ramps to accommodate the changes in elevation along the canal route. Plans for such a system had largely been discarded by this time, however.) The total cost of the canal was pegged at $6 million, or $20,000 per mile. Clinton estimated that it would take between 10 and 15 years to build the entire canal, but he noted that sections could be opened up as they were completed. This would allow revenue from tolls to begin coming in even before the canal was fully operational.

Meetings to rally local supporters were held up and down the valleys of central New York. The hue and cry for a canal grew louder. When the New York State legislature came into session in February 1816, the lawmakers could not ignore the tidal wave of support for a canal. Legislative opponents of the canal dragged the debate into the following year, but by April 17, 1816, the last day of the legislature's spring session, the canal bill finally was passed.

A new commission was chosen that included several familiar old faces—Clinton, Ellicott, and van Rensselaer, along with some new ones—Samuel Young and Myron Holley. Gouverneur Morris was not reselected. He died not long after, in November 1816. The new commission divided the length of the proposed route into three regional divisions and appointed an engineer for each division. James Geddes was assigned the western section.

In February 1817, the new commission made a report to the state legislature that described a planned canal of 353 miles in length, from Albany to Lake Erie. The canal was designed to be 40 feet across its top, with sides that tapered downward to 28 feet across at the bottom. Because it required no currents of moving water and had to accommodate only canal boats that drew little water, the canal would be four feet deep. Twenty-seven locks needed to be built. Each lock would be 90 feet long, 12 feet across and "sufficient to accommodate boats of 100 tons."[2] Construction would begin in the middle section of the canal, a length of 77 miles, where the work would be easiest because the landscape was nearly flat. That section would require the construction of only six locks. A revised cost per mile was developed. The new estimate was scaled down to $13,800 per mile, thereby reducing the estimated total construction cost to less than $5 million. In its report, the commission also included plans for a short canal from the northern end of the Hudson River to Lake Champlain at an estimated cost of $871,000. The commissioners hoped that the New York legislators would respond positively.

By March 18, 1817, a new canal bill was introduced on the legislative floor. In the bill, the commissioners once again raised the total estimated cost of canal construction from $5 to $6 million. After a month of debate, the Canal Law of 1817 was approved. This legislation created a canal fund to handle the monies for everything from administrative costs to building costs. To help raise money, the law established a tax on salt, steamboat travel, and on all property within 25 miles of the proposed canal. On July 1, 1817, after a special midterm election, DeWitt Clinton became governor of New York. Now, as the state's chief executive, he was in a position to give a new level of support to the canal.

GROUNDBREAKING

Nearly 100 years had passed since Cadwallader Colden had suggested, in vague detail, an improved waterway system across central New York. Now the time had come for construction to begin on a project more elaborate than anything Colden had imagined. Work began, officially, on July 4, 1817, just three days after Clinton's election as governor. A special ceremony was held near Rome, New York, at the headwaters of the Mohawk River, at sunrise, and ground was broken for the construction of what would become a 350-mile-long canal system across the state. The canal commissioners were present, as were many dignitaries and local residents. As the sun rose above the eastern horizon, cannon from the U.S. Arsenal at Rome were fired. If completed as planned, the canal would be the longest in America. During the ceremony, Governor Clinton jammed a shiny new shovel into the black New York dirt to signal the beginning of construction on the Erie Canal. Other commissioners followed suit. Immediately, a team of oxen hitched to a plow was whipped into action, and the first furrow was plowed out along the canal route.

Work on the Erie Canal was finally under way. The commissioners and the newly appointed regional engineers still had important decisions to make, however. During the eight years that followed, the engineers learned how to build the canal to fit the landscape, and "the canal became a school of engineering in itself."[3] There was no canal in existence in the world at that time that fit the profile of the canal being built across New York. European canals—Dutch, French, and English—generally had been built in places where significant populations already lived, and where the only forests were patches of trees scattered here and there. In New York, it was nearly impossible for canal workers to dig a single yard of canal bed without first having to remove a dozen or more trees. The region through which the Erie Canal was to pass "was so untamed when construction began that there was no scheduled stagecoach line west of the headwaters of the Mohawk at Rome, which meant that the stages traveled only 125 miles westward from Albany before turning back toward the Hudson."[4] Along the middle section of the canal route, between Utica and Rome, there were fewer than 10 villages in existence.

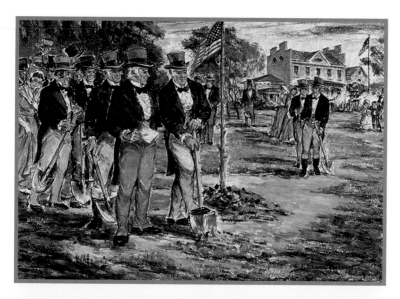

Referred to by skeptics as "Clinton's Folly," or "Clinton's Ditch," plans for the Erie Canal were quickly approved after Governor DeWitt Clinton took office. Above, Clinton and his commissioners marked the start of construction at the groundbreaking ceremony on July 4, 1817.

Although it would be years before the man-made waterway was completed, the commissioners called for the recognition of milestones along the way. In 1819, there was a lively celebration of the first boat to pass along the completed middle section of the canal. In 1823, festivities honored the uniting of the eastern portion of the canal to the Hudson River. Finally, in 1825, when the canal was completed, the greatest celebration of them all was held.

Between 1817 and 1820, to provide financing for the development and building of the canal, the commissioners sold investments through a series of canal loans. Small investors took out most of the loans. This meant that the canal was financed, not just by large corporate investors, but by small entrepreneurs who were willing to risk what they had because of their belief in the future of the canal. All loans taken out on the canal before 1822 paid out at 6 percent interest and were redeemable by 1837. There were larger investors, too. These included the Bank for Savings in New York City, which had control of 30 percent of all canal stock purchased by 1821. Other large investors included John Jacob Astor, who had made his initial fortune in the fur trade of the Far West, and other large financial houses, both in America and in England.

CONSTRUCTION ON THE MIDDLE SECTION

Work on the middle leg of the canal soon began, under the leadership of engineer Benjamin Wright. Wright wanted to see 1,000 men on the job by October 1817. James Geddes, who had made the original surveys in 1810, was responsible for designing many of the canal's mechanical structures. Geddes was in charge of the western section of the project. In the east, engineer-surveyor Charles Broadhead was in charge. The three men had help from a talented team of professionals. A Quaker engineer named David Thomas made maps of the route. Nathan S. Roberts, a surveyor turned engineer, laid out a significant portion of the canal line. He made his most important contribution, however, by designing the series of five "double combined locks" that were built side by side to carry canal boats over the 76 feet needed to surmount the rock ridge at Lockport. Roberts also trained John B. Jervis, another engineer on the Erie Canal project. All of these men and others made crucial contributions to the design and layout of the canal.

The construction of the Erie Canal, in all its various regional parts, relied on the skills of some of the greatest civil engineers of the early nineteenth century. One of those men was David Stanhope Bates, an assistant engineer on the canal who worked alongside Benjamin Wright. While working on the Erie Canal project, Bates furthered his reputation as an engineer of extraordinary skill, tireless energy, perseverance, good judgment, and the personal industry to see the work through.

David Stanhope Bates was born in New Jersey on June 10, 1777, on a small farm located between Morristown and Parsippany. As an adult, he appears to have had a nearly photographic memory for detail. In his work with others, he had the personal and professional skills necessary to communicate exactly what needed to be done.

In 1810, Bates was approached by a wealthy New Yorker named George Scriba, an immigrant from Scotland, to complete a survey of a large tract of land in New York's Oneida County. Bates and his family packed up and moved to a small frontier settlement on Oneida Lake, a place known today as Constantia, New York. In the summer of 1810, New York governor DeWitt Clinton and his canal commissioners examined the potential for canal construction along the Mohawk River Valley and westward across New York. During the next several years, as Bates continued his survey, his work became known to those who were organizing a canal effort. In 1817, Bates applied to Benjamin Wright—a man with whom he had worked many times on surveys across central New York State—for a job as an engineer on the Erie Canal. Wright named him as assistant engineer on the middle leg of the canal project.

THE CONTRIBUTIONS OF CANVASS WHITE

Another engineer who made a unique contribution to the canal project was Canvass White. White was born in 1790 and grew up on an Oneida County farm when that region was still frontier land. He was wounded during the War of 1812 while fighting as a lieutenant in the New York Volunteers. White was fascinated by all things mechanical, including the canal project. He had read Elkanah Watson's reports on British canals and believed that they did not tell the complete story. In 1817, he asked and received permission from Governor Clinton and Benjamin Wright to make a trip to England to examine the English canal system and report back with his findings. Perhaps, he thought,

CANVASS WHITE'S
VALUABLE CONTRIBUTION

As the canal project advanced, the engineers and construction crews generally relied on local materials in their work. The builders used local stone that was hauled to the canal site from short distances away. They also drew timber from local forests. They utilized locally acquired mud and limestone compounds to waterproof the canal's lining. This waterproofing proved to be more difficult to manage than had been expected. Through the work of engineer Canvass White, however, the problem was solved.

During the first year of construction, a key decision had to be made about the canal's locks: Should they be made of wood or of stone? Governor Clinton and the canal's chief engineers debated the subject long and hard. Wood was cheaper, but constant contact with water would cause it to rot in just a few years. Locks built with stone would be more permanent but posed a problem. The stones would need to be cemented together with hydraulic cement, a substance that was very expensive. The main ingredient in hydraulic cement—a volcanic rock called *trass*—was rare in America. When exposed to water, trass turned as hard as the stones it cemented in place. Unlike wood, it did not deteriorate in water. To import trass from England would be quite costly, however.

In 1818, as the debate between wood and stone continued, Canvass White returned from his trip to England. He had gone there in 1817, with Governor Clinton's encouragement, to study canal structures. White knew that trass was the key to using stone for the canal's locks. He also knew that trass had been discovered recently in Massachusetts. White suspected that trass also might be found in New York State, near the canal route. He

(continues)

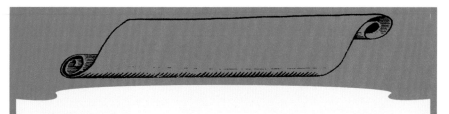

(continued)

began to comb the landscape in search of a deposit of trass. He found just what he was looking for near Chittenango, New York: a trasslike substance called meager limestone. Happily, Chittenango was located near the Erie Canal route. To make certain that he had found the right substance, White placed a piece of it in water overnight. The following morning, he found that it had become rock-hard, exactly as he had hoped. There was no longer any question about whether the canal locks would be made of wood or of stone.

The meager limestone was made into cement by calcining (heating) the stone, pulverizing it into a powder, and then adding it to sand and water. The resulting mixture was cement far superior to any other found in America at that time. It also had the advantage of becoming harder over constant exposure to water.

White's contribution to the canal project was invaluable. Beginning in 1819, the material he had advocated was used everywhere along the canal route that mortar was necessary. In all, 400,000 bushels of the meager limestone compound were used. White tried to take out a patent on his compound in 1820, but he was challenged immediately by the canal commissioners. Because all of White's work was done as a canal project employee, the commissioners considered his discovery to be theirs. When the commissioners tried to bypass White by encouraging the canal crews to make their own cement using White's basic system, White filed a suit against the canal builders. White won his suit and soon established a prosperous cement business that lasted until 1840. Throughout those years, White used the Erie Canal to ship his product as cheaply as possible.

he could bring back some of the tricks of the trade that the British had used to solve sticky canal problems. White did not return from his English trip until 1818. On the trip, he managed to walk along 2,000 miles of English canals and examine them in detail. The information he brought back proved extremely valuable to the other engineers on the Erie Canal.

In the meantime, surveyors were laying out the exact route of the canal. They marked it with two rows of red stakes spaced 60 feet apart. Inside those rows, they drove two rows of stakes spaced 40 feet apart. These inner stakes indicated the precise line of excavation. The 10-foot spaces between the inner and outer rows on each side of the canal showed the locations of the towpaths. After each section of the route was marked, a team of borers drove holes 12 feet deep to determine the composition of the soil underground. The borers were followed by the actual diggers and levelers. The surveyors soon realized that, for nearly 60 miles west of Rome, on the way to Utica, the land along the route lay almost level. The stretch became known as the Long Level. Construction began on the Long Level in January 1818.

When choosing construction workers, the canal commission at first relied on local farmers and mechanics, as well as merchants and skilled labor that lived close to the canal route. The commissioners avoided hiring foreign workers, especially those who were Irish. Eventually, especially in later years, a significant number of Irish immigrants would work on the canal, but they were nowhere close to a majority. An 1819 canal report shows that three-fourths of canal workers were native-born Americans. Most of the subsequent reports that exist today (the New York State Library in Albany is home to half a million such reports) show that most canal workers were local recruitments. They may have been the descendants of Irish immigrants, but they were not themselves from Ireland. Some workers were not locals, but men who simply moved from one section of the canal route to another in

Starting in Rome, New York, construction on the Erie Canal began with a large group of unskilled canal workers. After eight years of digging, excavating, and building without bulldozers or modern equipment, the canal was completed.

search of work as soon as their labors were no longer needed on a completed section.

THE HARD WORK OF CONSTRUCTION

Many of the jobs to be done on the canal were not much different from jobs that might be done on a farm. Just as on a farm, trees needed to be felled and streams needed to be diverted. Canal work was different from farm work in other ways, however. Canal laborers were employed by and worked for someone else, such as an on-site boss. Canal laborers also worked for wages.

The pay was adequate. Laborers received between $8 and $12 per month, or 50 cents per day. The men who contracted with the canal commissioners to organize crews to excavate the earth were paid 10 to 14 cents per cubic yard. Pay rates were higher for rock excavation. If the excavation was of loose marl, a contractor was paid 75 cents per cubic yard. If a crew was digging out breccia, a hard rock, the contractor might receive as much as $2 per cubic yard. Excavation along embankments paid 16 to 25 cents per yard, and locks and culverts paid out at 75 cents to $1.50. Such contracted amounts were quite generous. In some cases, they were so generous that contractors worked out deals with subcontractors who were willing to do the work more cheaply and pocketed the difference.

Wages and salaries for professional contributors to the canal project also were high. The principal engineers were paid an annual salary between $1,500 and $2,000. Assistant engineers were paid $4 per day. In 1819, commissioners began receiving $2,500 annually, but by 1820, this was lowered to $2,000.

Construction of the canal required massive amounts of material, and nearly all of it came from local sources. In addition to wood and stone, the engineers needed something to help make the canal bed as waterproof as possible. They relied initially on a muddish material called "the blue mud of the meadows" that proved to be serviceable in keeping water from seeping through the walls and bottom of the canal. In the vicinity of Medina, New York, the engineers found a variety of limestone that provided an excellent material for "facing" the locks and other places where good stone was needed. Then, engineers located a type of rock known as "meager limestone" that could be used as water cement (cement that hardens in water). Before the use of this substance, construction was slowed by a lack of good mortar to use with stone. The person responsible for introducing meager limestone to the canal project was Canvass White.

These innovations grew out of the canal commission's philosophy: Construct the canal out of the best available materials and build it to last as long as possible. To that end, the commissioners relied on stone and iron as frequently as possible and used wood, which would rot out in a short period of time, as sparingly as they could. The commissioners were especially interested in building locks as permanent structures. A 90-foot-by-15-foot lock cost approximately $1,000 for every foot of rise for a canal boat. The quality of lock materials is addressed in an 1819 report:

> The foundations of these . . . locks, are to consist of a solid flooring of hewed timber, one foot thick, and covered with well jointed three inch plank, over which, within the chamber, will be laid another flooring, of two inch plank, accurately fitted together with water joints, and spiked down, so as to prevent leakage: and this foundation is to be strongly supported and guarded by piling. The lock walls are to be sustained by several massy buttresses [sic], to be laid in water-cement, and thoroughly grouted—to have all the faces, ends, and beds of each stone, laid in front of the wall, together with the hollow quoins, the lock culverts and the ventilators, well cut—and the whole to be sufficiently cramped together with iron, and the best construction, and properly fitted, secured, and hung.[5]

The year 1819 was a difficult one for the canal builders. Little construction took place during wintertime, but materials were delivered up and down the canal route by sleigh. Normally, sleighs were even easier to use than wagons in summertime. In winter 1818–1819, however, the snows either fell too lightly or came as blizzards, making the use of sleighs almost impossible. (Winter weather continued to affect the canal after its completion. Typically, the canal closed down for

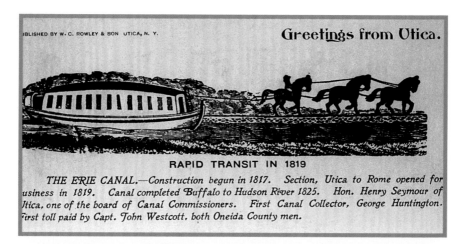

PUBLISHED BY W. C. ROWLEY & SON UTICA, N. Y.

Greetings from Utica.

RAPID TRANSIT IN 1819

THE ERIE CANAL.—Construction begun in 1817.   Section, Utica to Rome opened for business in 1819.   Canal completed Buffalo to Hudson River 1825.   Hon. Henry Seymour of Utica, one of the board of Canal Commissioners.   First Canal Collector, George Huntington. First toll paid by Capt. John Westcott. both Oneida County men.

In 1820, workers finished the middle section of the Erie Canal, which connected Utica to Rome. Traffic on that section started up immediately. Today, nearly 80 percent of upstate New York's population lives within 25 miles of the canal. Above is a postcard featuring the Utica section of the Erie Canal.

five months during most winters.) In the summer of 1819, the canal men were beset by heat, humidity, and mosquitoes. The crews often worked in marshy regions, where mosquitoes were a significant bother—and deadly. Approximately 1,000 canal workers became ill with a variety of fevers, primarily malaria. The disease must have been prevalent across New York State. DeWitt Clinton's wife, Maria, died of what probably was malaria in 1818. She contracted the disease while summering on Staten Island, near New York City.

The middle leg of the canal was completed by 1820. The inauguration of this part of the canal took place a bit earlier, however, on October 23, 1819. As part of that celebration, the commissioners and 50 or so dignitaries boarded a canal boat called the *Chief Engineer* to travel along the new man-made waterway from Utica to Rome. The boat was pulled by a single horse that walked the towpath along the canal. Church bells rang along the way as the boat and its passengers passed, and the fenced banks along the canal route were lined with throngs of cheering well-wishers.

Another celebration was held along this section of the canal on July 4, 1820, three years after the groundbreaking. On this occasion, a flotilla of 73 canal boats made its way through the waterway. As one newspaper reported, "To see the first boat launched, to be among the first that were borne on the waters of a canal which is to connect the great chain of western lakes with the Hudson . . . produced emotions which those only who felt them can conceive."[6]

The completion of the middle section opened up 94 miles of canal from Utica to Montezuma on the Seneca River. Although much of this stretch of the canal was built across largely level land, the challenges posed by the actual project answered most of the builders' questions about building a canal across central New York. Soon, this completed portion of the canal was busy with traffic, and small villages began to spring up along the route.

Locks and Aqueducts

When the first section of the Erie Canal opened, New Yorkers were introduced to the age of canals. Whole tracts of central New York suddenly were opened to new possibilities. For many residents of the area, the limits of living on the frontier suddenly were swept away. What had seemed impossible just a few years earlier had been achieved. Doubters and critics who had referred mockingly to "Clinton's Big Ditch" or "Clinton's Folly" were nearly all silenced by the successful construction of nearly 100 miles of canal. As the commissioners wrote in their 1820 report:

> The novelty of seeing large boats drawn by horses, upon waters artificially conducted—through cultivated fields, forests and swamps, over ravines, creeks and morasses, and

Though many did not believe it could be done, the opening of the first strip of the Erie Canal silenced the skeptics. Especially impressive were the locks *(above)* located throughout the canal, which allowed boats to travel from one level of the canal to another with a higher or lower elevation.

from one elevation to another, by means of ample, beautiful and substantial locks, has been eminently exhilarating [sic]. The precision of the levels, the solidity of the banks, the regularity of the curves, the symmetry of the numerous and massive stone works, the depth of the excavation in some places, the extent of the embankments in others, and the impression produced everywhere along the line, by the visible effects of immense labor, have uniformly afforded gratification mingled with surprise.[1]

These were words written by men who obviously were proud of their work. They had remade their state's landscape, enhancing its practicality, and the world of upstate New York would never be the same. So much confidence was placed in the canal project and its future worth that when the United States fell into a depression known as the Panic of 1819, work on the canal continued. The commissioners continued to raise money as if nothing was wrong with the economy, even as the cost of construction continued to rise. Between 1821 and 1824, the canal commissioners paid more than $1 million annually to contractors, and the average cost of a mile of canal construction grew to more than $26,000. In July 1820, the first tolls were collected on the canal. Six months later, nine additional miles along the canal's western section were completed and filled with water, and another 50 miles were approximately half-finished.

By 1820, work was underway on the eastern section of the canal. By the end of 1821, canal boats were in operation along a 24-mile stretch of canal between Utica and Little Falls, and significant progress was being made on work on the canal from the Falls to Albany. Tolls soon were being collected "on everything from salt, gypsum, grains, timber, and bricks to passenger boats charging 5 cents per mile."[2] Tolls collected in 1821 were five times greater than those collected in 1820. Even with the increase, however, the tolls collected in 1821 covered only 13 percent of the interest payments on the nearly $3 million in canal loans in existence.

WORKING ON THE WESTERN SECTION

West of the long Rome summit level, near Syracuse, the level of the completed middle section of the canal began to drop toward New York's lake country. There the canal passed along a lower summit between Nine Mile Creek and the Skaneateles Outlet on its way to the Seneca River. In this region, water fed into the canal from a variety of small streams. Where the western section began, the canal crossed over the Seneca River along a towpath bridge to the Cayuga marshes near the village of Lyons. Farther west, the canal received its water from the Genesee River, which lay at an elevation 130 feet higher than the Seneca. Here, nature lent a hand with a series of natural ridges that carried the water along the valley to the Cayuga marshes. These ridges had been discovered by James Geddes during his 1808 survey expedition. They would become the linchpin of the western length of the Erie Canal. The building of all of these segments took immense planning by the canal's engineers.

The work along this leg of the canal was complicated and difficult. Workers digging through the Cayuga marshes often labored in standing water a foot deep. In 1820 and 1821, fevers became commonplace. By the spring of 1822, the canal had been dug through the marshes. The canal reached Lyons, New York, in June of that year. A local newspaper reported "the successful execution of an undertaking, so arduous, so extensive, and in our country, so novel . . . and more than any thing else occupying the thoughts of a great community."[3]

Even as the canal builders made progress along the western section, the engineers faced a pair of unique engineering problems. First, the canal had to pass above the valley of Irondequoit Creek. Second, it had to cross the Genesee River. These were not easy problems, and their solutions would stretch the limits of canal engineering in that era.

Irondequoit Creek was misnamed. In truth, it was a river that was capable of carrying boats up to 30 tons in weight on their way to Lake Ontario. East of Rochester, the Irondequoit ran north at the bottom of a deep, narrow valley. It also cut a path across the east-west route of the canal. This was a serious problem:

> It was no simple matter to get a forty-foot-wide ditch full of
> water across a U-shaped chasm with about one mile between

the top of one side and the top of the other. The low point of the U varied from forty to seventy feet below the upper rims. Consequently, the slopes down to the creek were too steep and the valley itself too narrow to provide room for locks down one side and then back up the other side. How, then, could the crossing be established?[4]

Across the valley of Irondequoit Creek, the commissioners agreed with the engineers that a 60-foot-high aqueduct would have to be built to carry the canal for a quarter of a mile through the valley. At first, the engineers intended to build the aqueduct out of wood. They decided, however, that such a structure might not be strong enough to withstand the winds that often swept through the valley. They chose, instead, to build a huge embankment out of stone and earth. The embankment had to have a hole in its bottom, however, to allow Irondequoit Creek to continue flowing. Canal workers sank 900 twenty-foot log pilings deep into the soft ground across the bottom of the valley to support a 245-foot-long semicircular culvert to deliver Irondequoit Creek beneath the embankment.

Many of the workers on this project, including those working on the embankment and the culvert, were Irish, and it was here that the Irish workers made one of their most important contributions to the canal project. Three thousand Irishmen worked here under the watchful eye of a contractor named J.J. McShane. He was a former prizefighter who had worked on canal projects in Ireland. McShane employed a "jigger boss," a man who dispensed drinks of whiskey to the workers several times daily. The work along Irondequoit Creek was grueling and backbreaking. An immense amount of earth had to be moved to build up the embankment that would carry the canal over the valley. The work required horses and oxen, wheelbarrows and wagons, and picks and shovels as well as human sweat and toil. The Irish work crews labored through long days in the heat of the upstate New York summer of 1822. They even worked after sundown, by the light of bonfires. They finished the project by October 1822. The work had taken two years.

No sooner were the embankment, the culvert, and the canal finished when a great rainstorm blew across the valley, filling the canal. Boats soon were plying the canal eastward to Little Falls, and westbound boats soon arrived in the region on their way to Rochester. One of the earliest boats to arrive in Rochester from Utica, 152 miles to the east, delivered not goods, but people: 8 families numbering 60 people, each of whom had paid $1.50 to travel along the canal.

With the canal in operation in the region, the town of Rochester saw immediate growth. This was a pattern for settlements along the new Erie Canal. Rochester was established just before the War of 1812. With the advent of the canal Rochester became home to thousands of people. It was noted for its "spacious streets . . . well-furnished shops, and the bustle which continually pervades them."[5] By 1827, two years after the completion of the canal, Rochester's population hit 8,000, and the embankment across the Irondequoit became a tourist attraction "where people had to crane their necks to see the canal boats sailing along so far above them."[6] By 1850, Rochester was home to 36,000 inhabitants and boasted significant industry, including mills and iron foundries.

CROSSING THE GENESEE RIVER

The second great problem the canal engineers had to solve near Rochester was the crossing of the Genesee River. At this point, the river's current was quite fast, and the Genesee Falls were situated almost in the canal's path. As at other locations along the route, the engineers decided to build an aqueduct to carry the canal over the river. Work began on the aqueduct in 1821. The river was wide. The aqueduct crossed the equivalent of three New York City blocks and was supported by nine Roman-style stone arches, each covering a 50-foot span. A pair of additional, smaller arches was added at each end. This made

Building the Erie Canal through Rochester was difficult for canal engineers, as the Upper Falls of the Genesee River added to the speed of the river current. An aqueduct was built, elevating the canal above the river and across Rochester.

the Genesee Aqueduct the largest aqueduct built to accommodate the Erie Canal.

The chief engineer on the Genesee Aqueduct project was William Britton. He recently had completed construction on another New York building project, a new state prison at Auburn. In an effort to pay his workers less and pocket more money for himself, Britton asked for and was given 28 prisoners to work as stonecutters to carve the stones for the arches. He brought in more convicts later to do additional work. This proved to be a bad idea. The workers had to be guarded at all times, and several escaped. When Britton died, during the winter of 1821–1822, the prisoner-worker program ended.

Other problems plagued the Genesee Aqueduct project. Local sandstone was delivered from the town of Medina for use on the arches. The red stone was not strong enough to carry the weight of the canal bridge across the river, however. Local engineers had to bring in limestone from 50 miles away at Lake Cayuga. Too few local workers were available, so, again, canal planners had to bring in Irish immigrant labor. Despite harsh winters (during the winter of 1821–1822, an ice floe destroyed one of the piers that held the arches) and rainy summers, the Genesee Aqueduct was finished by September 1823. It was almost a year behind schedule and $83,000 over budget.

The results, however, were phenomenal. The aqueduct spanned the great, rolling river through a region that recently had been little more than frontier wilderness. The elevated waterway was capable of holding 2,000 tons of water and 200 tons of boats and cargo. Great celebrations were held that October, when "a cluster of colorful boats gathered, the bands played, the orators orated, the clergymen sermonized, and the highest-ranking notables enjoyed a lavish feast at a local tavern, washed down with twenty-five toasts."[7] During the celebrations, oysters were delivered by canal boat to Rochester. The oysters came from New York City. Oysters had never been available in the region, but the canal delivered them over the 450 miles from the Atlantic so quickly that they were still fresh.

Even as cargoes of oysters reached Rochester from the east, a cargo of 10,000 barrels of flour left Rochester, headed toward New York City. All of this took place within the first 10 days of the canal's opening. In the years that followed, Rochester, with its mills powered by the Genesee Falls, gained the nickname "Flour City." During the first year of canal operations in Rochester, the local canal authorities collected nearly $10,000 in tolls.

Despite all the fanfare and celebration that accompanied the completion of the Genesee Aqueduct, however, the structure proved inadequate in operation. Because it was too narrow to allow canal boats to pass one another, there were long waits and arguments over which boats should have the right of way. The aqueduct also began to leak seriously. By 1833, another aqueduct had to be constructed.

CONSTRUCTION ALONG THE EASTERN SECTION

Building the canal along the eastern section also had its problems. East of Utica, the land fell approximately 105 feet in just 8 miles. Farther east, on the 86-mile stretch between Little Falls and the Hudson River, the land rose and fell sharply and repeatedly. Near Little Falls, "the landscape . . . was the most defiant in the entire valley."[8] The canal had to be excavated between steep banks, some of which rose as high as 500 feet. This necessitated the construction of 13 locks in close order between Little Falls and Schenectady.

Building the canal became even more difficult east of Schenectady. There, the land dropped 200 feet in 16 miles. This necessitated the building of 27 locks, a number equal to one-third of the lock construction required along the full length of the Erie Canal. Continuing farther east, the engineers tried to build the canal along the south bank of the Mohawk River. The river twisted and turned so frequently, however, and the banks became so steep, that the engineers realized that they would have to cross and re-cross the river several times. To solve this problem, the engineers devised an ingenious strategy. They built two long aqueducts, one to carry the canal from the south bank to the north bank of the river and another to deliver the canal back from the north to the south. These proved to be impressive pieces of canal architecture. The aqueduct built near Schenectady measured 748 feet in length, with 16 pillars providing support. On it, canal boats traveled above the raging

REINVENTING TREE REMOVAL

Each day at the canal-building sites, the workers faced a multitude of problems. One of the biggest was what to do about thousands of tree stumps. Much of the canal was built through thick woods. The trees were cut down, leaving stumps behind. These stumps were large and difficult to remove; digging them out by hand was nearly impossible. During the building of the Erie Canal, some inventive canal workers devised and built a stump-puller, a large-wheeled machine. The stump-puller had two 16-foot-wide drum wheels and an axle that measured 20 inches in diameter and 30 feet in length. A cable attached to the axle was anchored tightly around a stump; the other end of the cable was attached to a drum wheel. A team of horses turned the giant drum wheel causing the cable to wrap around the drum and pull the stump from its root base. The whole operation required a six-man crew and a team of large, powerful horses. The stump-puller was capable of removing as many as 40 stumps in a long, busy day.

Other innovations made the work of building the canal easier. Even before the canal was completed, a more efficient and powerful stump-puller was developed. A heavy cable was attached to the high part of a tall tree, and by winding an endless screw, one worker was able to remove a stump single-handedly. To clear the underbrush from the canal site, a pair of cutting blades were attached to a plow. With this contraption, a worker could plow a site and prepare it for digging while cutting the underbrush at the same time.

river at a height of 30 feet. The second aqueduct was built above Cohoes Falls to return the canal to the Mohawk's south bank. This immense structure measured 1,188 feet and was supported by 26 piers. It would be the longest of the 18 aqueducts required in building the canal. These two aqueducts were built between 1823 and 1824. Both aqueducts required great engineering skill, and they ultimately saved the commissioners $75,000 in construction expenses, "or nearly 30 percent of what it would have cost to go all the way on the south side of the river."[9]

In all, the eastern section of the canal between Schenectady and Albany cost $540,000, and most of that amount was required to build the 16 miles between Schenectady and Troy. Compared with the cost of canal construction between the Seneca River and Utica, the Schenectady-to-Albany section cost twice as much per mile. In late 1824, when the entire canal section between Utica and the Hudson was finished, the commissioners breathed a sigh of relief. Their annual report stated that, if construction on the canal had begun exclusively along the eastern section, the engineers might have abandoned the project completely because they would not have had the experience and knowledge gained during construction of the middle section. The same report estimated that "the completion of the project would have been postponed for as long as a hundred years."[10]

As soon as the eastern section, with its 27 locks between Schenectady and Albany, opened, canal traffic became heavy. The canal ran 24 hours a day, and canal boat crews often had to endure long waits. A trip on the canal between these two points took at least 24 hours and lasted even longer when too many boats were in use. Because of the amount of time required to traverse this section of the canal, nearly all of the boats carried heavy cargoes and few passengers. After all, passengers could reach Schenectady from Albany in three hours by stagecoach for less than $1 a ticket.

Building the Western Canal

The fall of 1823 marked significant progress in the construction of the Erie Canal. By October 1, the entire eastern section of the canal was completed, and celebrations soon were under way in Rochester. Canal boats now could ply the man-made waterway for 250 miles between Albany and the Genesee River Valley. With the opening of the canal to the Hudson River, the combined natural and artificial waterway stretched for 375 miles, connecting the Atlantic Ocean to Rochester. Little Falls had been conquered, the embankment at Iron-dequoit was completed, and the Genesee Aqueduct was on line, all having presented significant engineering obstacles. The secondary canal between the Hudson River and Lake Champlain was finished and open for business. This canal was short, just 64 miles, but it had required 12 locks. At its lake end was the small village of Whitehall; at its southern end was the town of

Watervliet, just seven miles north of Albany. Watervliet was home to a federal arsenal that had opened in 1813. Now the town also served as the junction of the two canals.

A great celebration was held in Albany on October 1 to mark the opening of both the east-west canal and the north-south waterway. A military band made up of cadets from the United States Military Academy at West Point was on hand, as were the usual orators. There were booming cannon salutes. So many people came out for the celebration and to see canal boats pass along their part of the canal that they lined the waterway's banks for miles. DeWitt Clinton was on hand, of course, and he arrived at the festivities on a packet boat that bore his name.

CHALLENGES ON THE WESTERN SECTION

Much of the canal was open, but completing the western section presented serious problems. Questions remained even about the basic route west of Rochester. The shortest and most direct route would have taken this leg of the canal out of Rochester in a southwesterly direction to Buffalo. The landscape along this route rose 75 feet above the level of Lake Erie, however. This meant that the lake could not be tapped as a water source for the canal. Other local streams did not contain enough water to service the canal, further complicating the direct route.

There was another option, however. The canal could follow a path west out of Rochester, remaining close to Lake Ontario for approximately 70 miles. The canal then could make a 90-degree turn to the south and reach Lake Erie in another 30 miles. Along this route, between Rochester and the turn, the canal would cross over relatively flat territory, and no locks would be needed. Lake Erie and Tonawanda Creek could be tapped to provide water for the canal. The turn itself would bring the canal to a stopping point, however. It also would be impossible to bypass the enormous Niagara Escarpment that rose up along the landscape between Rochester and Lake Erie.

The escarpment was directly in this route's path and would require the canal to climb up 70 feet over solid rock. Given the water supply issues, however, this was the only viable solution for a route to Buffalo.

The commissioners took proposals for the daunting project from various engineers. They finally chose a proposal submitted by staff engineer Nathan S. Roberts, a 46-year-old New Yorker who had grown up near Canastota. He had been the chief engineer on the section of the canal between Rome and Syracuse. Roberts's solution to the problem was to cut a series of locks straight out of the escarpment, one after the other, like a flight of stairs. Such lock "stairs" already had been built on the canal, but Roberts's plan was on a larger scale than had been attempted before. He had to redesign the size of the locks to fit his plan. He designed a series of 5 double locks, each of which measured 12 feet in height rather than the standard 8 feet, 4 inches, used on all other locks on the Erie project. The fact that Roberts also designed these as double locks meant that there were 2 locks at each level, for a total of 10, so that canal boats could be lowered and raised at the same time in separate lock structures. This would keep the traffic moving.

Roberts's plan did not deliver the canal to the very top of the escarpment, however. The rock formation continued on for another 10 feet and loomed even higher above the fifth lock. Using survey information that he had gathered himself in combination with the information from James Geddes's survey, Roberts knew that the west side of the escarpment dropped slightly but inevitably. Roberts intended to cut "right into the solid rock face to sculpt a channel carrying the canal, and a towpath beside it for seven miles in a straight line southward to the town of Pendleton."[1] From there, the canal would connect with Tonawanda Creek, which flowed slowly toward the southwest into the Niagara River adjacent to Lake Erie, entering the river just 10 miles north of Buffalo.

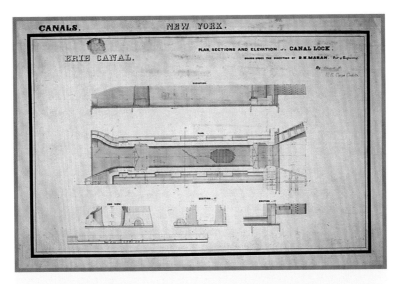

In order to build the canal through New York State, the engineers had to configure a series of locks to allow boats to travel from one elevation to another. By guiding a boat in between two gates, both of which control the water level inside the lock, ships could be easily lowered or lifted to another section of the canal. *Above*, a sketch design of an Erie Canal lock.

WORK BEGINS AT LOCKPORT

Construction began on Roberts's plan at a site 18 miles south of Lake Ontario, just north of a small hamlet occupied by only three families. The tiny community was soon nicknamed "Lockport." By January 1823, the settlement had become home to more than 300 canal workers and their families. Before the work at Lockport was completed, two and a half years later, the local population had swelled to 3,000 residents and 2,000 canal workers who worked on the locks and on the Deep Cut, the channel Roberts designed to run across the top of the Niagara Escarpment. The majority of these canal workers were Irish, and many of them made Lockport their home long after the canal project was completed.

Work on the Deep Cut took much labor and involved work with explosives. These were used to cut through the escarpment's ancient, hard rock. Work on the cut began south of Lockport, at a site 13 feet below the top of the escarpment. Through the first mile and a half of the cut, the escarpment rose ever higher; the trough hacked and blasted out by the workers ran 30 feet deep. Beyond that point, the rock mountain descended gradually to Tonawanda Creek. The rock was defiant. It was so hard that, when workers tried to drill holes for blasting, their drill bits broke. Only after a local resident discovered a means to temper, or harden, the steel drill bits were the workers able to make the appropriate blast holes.

The blasts of gunpowder created their own problems. A blast threw so much rock, and threw it so far, that pieces fell on the streets of Lockport. Young boys were hired to light the powder charge fuses because the boys could sprint to safety faster than grown men. All of the rock debris—great scatterings of stones in various sizes—had to be removed from the site. Much of this work was done with large wooden-beamed derricks, the great booms of which swung buckets down to the bottom of the cut. There, workers filled them with rock debris. Horses then pulled the derrick cables to raise the buckets of rock up and out of the cut. The cut was completed in October 1824, a year before the canal was fully operational.

When explosives were used in the construction of the canal, there were accidents. The blasts sometimes killed workers. Some were killed by the explosions themselves; others were killed by flying debris. Throughout the project, in fact, no work on the canal was completely safe. There were accidents of all sorts. Canal beds caved in, burying or smothering canal workers. Some men fell to their deaths from cliffs and embankments; others toppled into dry lock chambers or aqueducts. A newspaper in Lockport reported on the death of a worker named Orrin Harrison. While working on the stairway of locks,

Harrison "was leaning against one of the balance beams, and from excessive fatigue fell asleep, and was precipitated into one of the locks, in about 8 feet of water."[2] Harrison's leg became trapped in the lock gates. Because he could not swim or climb out of the lock, he drowned.

In 1824, as the work at Lockport and Rochester continued, other work was under way along other sections of the canal route. In that year, canal workers built 300 bridges over the canal to rejoin farmlands and other properties that had been bisected by the canal. The canal junction at Tonawanda Creek was completed. Special scales were installed at Utica, Syracuse, and Troy to weigh canal boats and their cargoes, so that accurate tolls could be assessed. The scales worked by measuring the amount of water displaced by a boat sitting in the water. At various lock sites, finishing touches were added to complete additional parts of the canal.

Once the work at Lockport was finished, the five stairstep locks were a wonder to behold. In a few short years, the site became a tourist attraction. Visitors flocked from all over the eastern United States and even came from Europe. As one visitor, a Canadian who saw the "Lockport Fives" in 1826, wrote:

> Lockport is itself a plain looking little village, but is rendered famous by its locks, of which there are 5 double ones upon the Canal, as close together as possible: as Niagara Falls are the greatest natural wonder, so Lockport, its Locks, and the portion of the Canal adjacent, are considered to be the greatest artificial curiosity in this part of America."[3]

Such tourists, as well as those who rode the canal as passengers, found that a canal trip could involve a certain amount of elegance. They rode the canal on passenger boats known as packets. Each measured 78 feet in length and 14.5 feet across. Each packet could carry 120 passengers. At the center of the

The sharp elevation in Niagara County needed a series of locks instead of one, and men from New York City were recruited for construction work. With the promise of work, wages, food, and whiskey, Irish immigrants were lured to the area and settled there permanently while building the "Flight of Five." *Above*, one of the five locks located in Lockport, New York.

boats were central cabins. By day, these "served as sitting rooms, with carpeted floors, stuffed chairs, and mahogany tables stacked high with newspapers and books."[4]

Some packets featured entertainment. Captains hired musicians and encouraged the passengers to dance on deck. Mealtimes were near feasts as a boat's crew turned the large central cabin into a dining hall and served up dinners of roast beef, ham, plum pudding, and liqueurs. At nightfall, the large cabin became yet another type of room as servants divided it into sleeping quarters. A central curtain divided the two halves of the cabin into ladies' and gentlemen's quarters. Along the outer walls, tiered berths were pulled down. These berths were tiered perhaps four deep, and were made up with sheets and blankets.

JOBS ON THE ERIE CANAL

The royal treatment received by passengers on the Erie Canal was made possible only through the work of canal employees, each of whom made his own unique contribution. All kinds of people with all kinds of skills found work on the canal. During the peak years of the Erie Canal's operation, a workforce of 25,000 people was needed to run the canal. These included lockkeepers, drivers, steersmen, and other workers. Both skilled and unskilled labor was necessary to keep the canal open and running smoothly and on time.

Many of those employed on the canal were young boys called hoggies (pronounced hawgeez). These boys held a variety of low-paying jobs on the canal, but many worked as canal boat drivers. Because canals, unlike rivers, did not have their own currents, canal boats had to be pulled along. A hoggy walked along the bank of the canal on the towpath, leading the horse or mule that pulled the canal boat. The work was difficult for the boys, who often had to sleep outdoors. Even when the weather brought rain, sleet, or hail, the hoggies had to stay on the job because the

(continues on page 108)

THE CANAL MEMORIALIZED IN SONG

Sometimes, the canal bisected the lands of local farms, and the farmers needed bridges to get from one field to another. These bridges were usually simple footbridges, built as cheaply as possible and extending just above the canal. They often were built so low that passengers on the decks of canal boats had to lean over or lie down as the boats passed under these bridges. Canal boat captains had to keep a watchful eye. They warned passengers of the approach of a footbridge by shouting, "Low bridge! Everybody down!" The words eventually found their way into a famous song.

Thomas S. Allen wrote the song "Fifteen Miles on the Erie Canal" in 1905, after the motive power for the canal's barge traffic had been converted from mule or horse power to modern steam engines. The use of engines increased the speed of canal boats to 15 miles a day. Allen's song is a memorial to the years between 1825 and 1880, when the canal became a success and made upstate communities such as Utica, Rome, Syracuse, Rochester, and Buffalo into successful canal towns.

Several versions of the song are known today, and they go by various titles: "Low Bridge, Everybody Down," "The Erie Canal Song," "Fifteen Years on the Erie Canal," "Mule Named Sal," and "Fifteen Miles on the Erie Canal." The version that follows is titled "Low Bridge, Everybody Down."

> I've got an old mule and her name is Sal
> Fifteen miles on the Erie Canal
> She's a good old worker and a good old pal
> Fifteen miles on the Erie Canal
> We've hauled some barges in our day

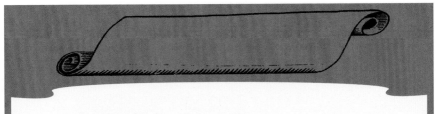

Filled with lumber, coal, and hay
And every inch of the way we know
From Albany to Buffalo

Chorus:
Low bridge, everybody down
Low bridge for we're coming to a town
And you'll always know your neighbor
And you'll always know your pal
If you've ever navigated on the Erie Canal

We'd better get along on our way, old gal
Fifteen miles on the Erie Canal
'Cause you bet your life I'd never part with Sal
Fifteen miles on the Erie Canal
Git up there mule, here comes a lock
We'll make Rome 'bout six o'clock
One more trip and back we'll go
Right back home to Buffalo

Chorus

Oh, where would I be if I lost my pal?
Fifteen miles on the Erie Canal
Oh, I'd like to see a mule as good as Sal
Fifteen miles on the Erie Canal
A friend of mine once got her sore
Now he's got a busted jaw

(continues)

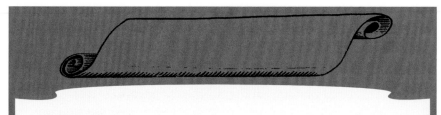

(continued)

> 'Cause she let fly with her iron toe
> And kicked him in to Buffalo
>
> *Chorus*
>
> Don't have to call when I want my Sal
> Fifteen miles on the Erie Canal
> She trots from her stall like a good old gal
> Fifteen miles on the Erie Canal
> I eat my meals with Sal each day
> I eat beef and she eats hay
> And she ain't so slow if you want to know
> She put the "Buff" in Buffalo
>
> *Chorus*

The song has remained popular over the past century, especially among folk singers. Those who recorded it during the 1950s and 1960s alone included Glenn Yarborough, Pete Seeger, the Weavers, the Kingston Trio, and the Sons of the Pioneers. The song sometimes shows up on recordings of children's songs. Even rock giant Bruce Springsteen included this musical tribute to the Erie Canal on his 2006 CD, *We Shall Overcome: The Seeger Sessions.*

(continued from page 105)

canal boats needed to stay on schedule. The boys were not paid very well for their labor, either; many earned no more than $30 for an entire canal season of seven to nine months.

As the hoggy kept a canal boat moving along the canal, another important figure manned the helm. Each canal boat had a steersman who kept the boat moving in a straight line. He remained at the boat's stern, or rear, and handled the boat's tiller bar. This was a wooden handle attached to the boat's rudder; the rudder, in turn, was a flat piece of wood that extended into the water at the back of the boat. When turned, the rudder steered the boat one way or the other. The steersman's job was important. If a canal boat was allowed to brush against or run into the side of the canal or into a bridge, a lock wall, or any other obstacle, the collision could do serious damage to the boat. Steersmen who steered their boats into lock walls or bridges were fined by canal officials.

The Canal Completed

On October 26, 1825, thousands of well-wishers gathered in Buffalo for a great dedication to mark the Erie Canal's opening. It was a stirring day, with a military band on hand, booming cannon, and several speeches. Governor Clinton was, of course, present. Having supported the building of the canal from the beginning, he had come to be known as the "Father of the Erie Canal." Clinton made a grand entrance to the celebrations; he arrived in Buffalo on his own specially made canal boat, the *Seneca Chief*. He then led 5,000 people down the streets of Buffalo.

CANNON ANNOUNCE THE CANAL

During the dedication, a succession of cannon was fired. Each cannon took its cue from the previous firing. With each consecutive blast, the word of the official dedication of the completed canal traveled from town to town. Cannon roared along the full length of the canal, from Buffalo to Albany. Cannon then boomed down the Hudson River to Sandy Hook, New Jersey, and along the southern banks of New York Harbor, where the final cannon was fired. Many of the cannon used in this celebratory relay had been captured from the British by Commodore Oliver Hazard Perry at the Battle of Lake Erie, during the War of 1812. The entire process of firing cannon between Buffalo and New York City took 80 minutes. Then, in reply, the cannon were fired again, all the way back up the Hudson and on to Buffalo. As one eyewitness later wrote, "Who that has American blood in his veins can hear this sound without emotion? Who that has the privilege to do it, can refrain from exclaiming, I too, am an American citizen; and feel as much pride in being able to make the declaration, as ever an inhabitant of the eternal city felt, in proclaiming that he was a Roman."[1] The eyewitness who wrote those words was Cadwallader Colden, the grandson and namesake of the surveyor who had suggested a canal across New York State a century earlier.

Following the special dedication, Governor Clinton and a handpicked group of people traveled along the entire length of the canal. The procession began at nine o'clock on the morning of October 26, with a parade led by the grand master himself, the governor. Clinton and others then boarded the packet *Seneca Chief*, which was pulled by four gray horses specially decorated for the celebration. Onboard the *Seneca Chief* was a pair of elegantly carved wooden kegs bearing eagle motifs and filled with water from Lake Erie. The *Seneca Chief* left Buffalo in the company of a small flotilla of boats that included, in order, the *Superior*, the *Buffalo*, an unnamed freight boat, and the *Commodore Perry*. Behind these craft came a long line of additional boats, including one that had been christened *Noah's Ark*. It carried an assortment of animals from western New York, all bound for New York City. The Ark's passengers included birds, a bear, two eagles, two fawns, several fish, and a pair of American Indian boys in native costume.

During the eight days that followed, the boats passed through the canal's many locks, and everyone onboard enjoyed their time on the waterway they had helped to make a reality. Many of those on the governor's boat, the *Seneca Chief*, were politicians and others who had supported the construction of the canal. All along the route, in every little village and hamlet, Clinton and his party were hailed. Not far from Syracuse, at the tiny town of Port Byron (then called Bucksville), the townspeople set off fireworks and fired many celebratory musket shots. They even launched an illuminated balloon, which the wind fortunately carried to the east, along the canal route. There was a great banquet, complete with a whole roasted ox, and the dinner was followed by many toasts and a dance.

The flotilla arrived in Albany, the state capital, on November 3. There, the boats, including Clinton's, were tied together, and a Hudson River steamboat pulled the string of boats downriver to New York City. Thousands of New Yorkers gathered along the river to cheer the arrival of their governor. In New York Harbor, Governor Clinton made a great symbolic gesture. Standing at Sandy Hook, he emptied the kegs filled with water from Lake Erie into the Atlantic Ocean. The Erie Canal had finally brought these natural waterways together in a "marriage of the waters." At last, after eight years of construction, the first boats had traveled the Erie Canal from end to end and then gone down the Hudson. The great American waterway soon became one of the most popular canals in the country.

THE CANAL HELPS AMERICA GROW

The canal had cost $7 million to construct and had required the building of 18 aqueducts and 83 locks, but it proved well worth its cost. Following the opening of the completed Erie Canal, the

Lake Erie town of Buffalo, New York, became the busiest lake port in America. As more and more people moved west, the canal carried midwestern trade goods back along the canal to the great port at New York City. Steamboats and sailing vessels traveled across the Great Lakes to deliver farm products to the Buffalo entrance of the canal. From the canal's eastern end, thousands of Americans and newly arrived immigrants headed west, using the canal as their major access route to such frontier territories and states as Ohio, Indiana, Illinois, and Michigan. The canal became vitally important to western migration and the development of the frontier: It delivered more Americans into the West during the 1830s and 1840s than any other western route, either overland or on water. Within five years of the canal's completion, 1,000 people per day were arriving in Buffalo by canal.

One of the greatest advantages brought about by the canal was the ability to ship goods cheaply. Before the Erie Canal, anyone shipping goods between Buffalo and New York City paid $100 per ton of freight, and the trip took three weeks. With the advent of the canal, water-borne freight rates dropped to $10 per ton, and the trip took only a week. In 1826 alone, 185,000 tons of farm products were shipped on the canal. These products included wheat, corn, flour, butter, cheese, potatoes, apples, whiskey, and livestock. In 1845, 1 million tons of freight was shipped on the Erie Canal. By the time of the Civil War (1861–1865), canal freight had increased to 3 million tons annually.

During the first decades of the Erie Canal's operation, the size of canal boats increased dramatically. The boats used on the canal from 1817 to 1830 were 61 feet long, 7 feet wide, and 3.5 feet deep. These early boats carried loads of up to 30 tons. By 1850, canal boats were 90 feet long and 15 feet wide and carried 100 tons. By 1862, the boats measured nearly 100 feet long and 17.5 feet wide.

Upon its completion, the Erie Canal connected five major cities of New York State together: Syracuse, Rochester, Buffalo, Utica, and Albany. The waterway allowed merchants to shuttle their goods throughout the state faster and more cheaply than ever before. The canal grew so popular, it has been enlarged twice since it was unveiled in 1825. *Above*, grain elevators along the Erie Canal in Buffalo.

AMERICA'S CANAL-BUILDING CRAZE

The Erie Canal proved to be so successful, so quickly, that its success inspired the construction of dozens of canals across the United States. During the 1820s alone, more than 800 miles of canals were constructed and opened for business along the Atlantic seaboard. States such as New York, Maryland, Delaware, and Pennsylvania all built significant canal systems.

THE ERIE CANAL INTO THE 21ST CENTURY

Throughout the nineteenth century, the Erie Canal remained one of the busiest waterways in America. It proved so popular, in fact, that a new Erie Canal was built between 1835 and 1862—one that was wider, deeper, and with double locks along its entire length to speed boats along. Canal authorities continued to collect tolls until 1882. By then, $42 million in tolls had been collected since the canal's opening.

The Erie Canal continues to be used today, if not in the same ways for which it was originally built. In 1905, it was renamed the Erie Barge Canal. It then was enlarged and reopened in 1918 under another new name, the New York Barge Canal. During the decades that followed, improvements, additions, and further enlargements took place. By the dawn of the 1990s, however, much of the original Erie Canal had fallen into disrepair and been abandoned. Then, in 1992, the New York State legislature created the New York State Canal Corporation for the purpose of refurbishing much of the old, historical canal. The corporation approved more than $30 million in 1996 to improve the old canal line for recreation, to allow private boats to use the old canal line, and to build hundreds of miles of biking and hiking trails along the Erie Canal's old towpaths.

Building these man-made waterways put thousands of canal builders and diggers to work. Between 1826 and 1827, more than 8,000 men were at work on just six canal projects. By the end of the decade, more than 1,300 miles of canals were being built. Ten years later, a total of 4,000 miles of canals had been completed.

The age of canals in America did not last forever, however. Just as the great canal-building phase was hitting its stride, a new form of transportation was introduced in the United States—the railroad. Canals were constructed because they allowed people and freight to travel where the nation's natural waterways did not go. Railroads did the same thing, but they were much less costly to build and maintain. Trains also traveled much faster than canal boats. The competition from railroads soon proved too much for the canals. By the 1840s, many canal projects were canceled before they were built. A number of existing canals went out of business. Some canals under construction were abandoned. In New York, however, when the Utica and Schenectady Railroad was completed in 1836, the state legislature passed a law forbidding the new rail line to carry freight. This was to prevent the railroad from competing with the Erie Canal.

Although canals are still used in America, their importance generally is less significant than it was during the early nineteenth century. During the era of America's westward migration, canals served as an important transportation system. These man-made waterways helped to define a period in United States history by delivering people and goods across the great, open expanses of the American landscape—and no canal made a greater mark on the pages of America's history than the Erie Canal.

Chronology

1609   English sea captain Henry Hudson, sailing for the Dutch, reaches the mouth of the Hudson River and sails up to present-day Albany.

1724   New York's surveyor general, Cadwallader Colden, suggests augmented navigation of a waterway across central New York State.

1768   New York governor Sir Henry Moore proposes improvement of New York's inland navigation. Nothing is done as immediate follow-up.

1777   Gouverneur Morris suggests a water route to deliver boats from the Hudson River to Lake Erie.

1784   Christopher Colles appears before the New York State legislature with an idea for a western water route across the state. The legislators show limited interest.

1788   A supporter of canals, Elkanah Watson, suggests a waterway that will become the Erie Canal. New York's legislators approve the creation of the Western Inland Lock Navigation Company and appoint Watson to its board.

1790s   The Western Inland Company completes limited canal work on the Mohawk River, including a few locks.

1803   New York State surveyor general Simeon DeWitt and Gouverneur Morris discuss the possibility of a canal across New York.

1808   Upstate New York businessman Jesse Hawley proposes a canal to link Lake Erie with the Hudson River.

1810   The New York legislature appoints a seven-man canal commission.

1811   The canal commission is authorized by the state legislature to buy out the old Western Inland Company and arrange financing for a new canal project.

1812   The state legislature authorizes the canal commission to borrow $5 million to lay groundwork for a canal.

1812-1815   The War of 1812 with Great Britain causes postponement of the canal project.

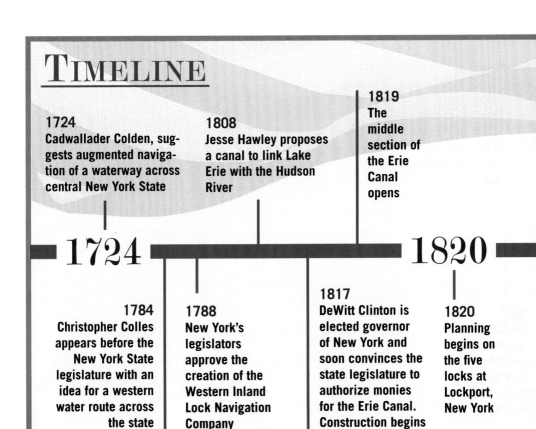

TIMELINE

1724
Cadwallader Colden, suggests augmented navigation of a waterway across central New York State

1808
Jesse Hawley proposes a canal to link Lake Erie with the Hudson River

1819
The middle section of the Erie Canal opens

1724   1820

1784
Christopher Colles appears before the New York State legislature with an idea for a western water route across the state

1788
New York's legislators approve the creation of the Western Inland Lock Navigation Company

1817
DeWitt Clinton is elected governor of New York and soon convinces the state legislature to authorize monies for the Erie Canal. Construction begins

1820
Planning begins on the five locks at Lockport, New York

1817   DeWitt Clinton is elected governor of New York and soon convinces the state legislature to authorize monies for the Erie Canal. Construction begins.

1819   The middle section of the Erie Canal, between Rome, New York, and Utica, New York, opens. The Champlain Canal opens between the Hudson River and Lake Champlain.

1820   Planning begins on the five locks at Lockport, New York.

1823   The Genesee Aqueduct is completed. Work begins on the "Lockport Fives."

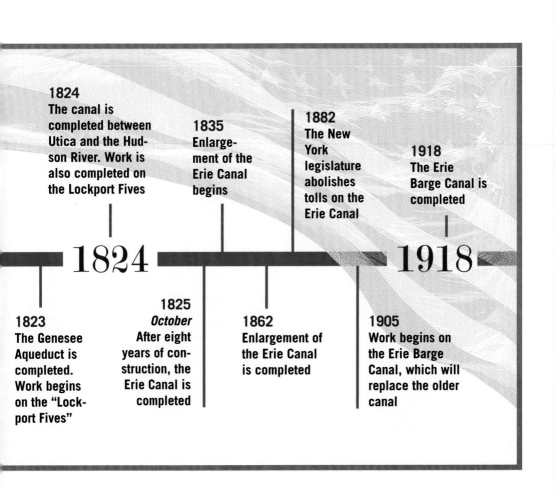

1824
The canal is completed between Utica and the Hudson River. Work is also completed on the Lockport Fives

1835
Enlargement of the Erie Canal begins

1882
The New York legislature abolishes tolls on the Erie Canal

1918
The Erie Barge Canal is completed

1824   **1918**

1823
The Genesee Aqueduct is completed. Work begins on the "Lockport Fives"

1825
October
After eight years of construction, the Erie Canal is completed

1862
Enlargement of the Erie Canal is completed

1905
Work begins on the Erie Barge Canal, which will replace the older canal

1824 The canal is completed between Utica and the Hudson River. Work is also completed on the Lockport Fives.

1825 **June** Hosted by DeWitt Clinton, the Marquis de Lafayette visits the Erie Canal.

October After eight years of construction, the Erie Canal is completed.

1835 Enlargement of the Erie Canal begins.

1862 Enlargement of the Erie Canal is completed.

1882 The New York legislature abolishes tolls on the Erie Canal.

1905 Work begins on the Erie Barge Canal, which will replace the older canal.

1918 The Erie Barge Canal is completed.

1996 The New York State Canal Corporation earmarks $32 million to alter the Erie Barge Canal for recreational use.

NOTES

CHAPTER 1

1. Peter L. Bernstein, *Wedding of the Waters: The Erie Canal and the Making of a Great Nation.* New York: W.W. Norton, 2005, 308.
2. Ibid.
3. Ibid., 309.

CHAPTER 2

1. James Kirby Martin, et al., *America and Its People.* New York: HarperCollins, 1993, 268.

CHAPTER 3

1. Bernstein, 49.
2. Ibid., 51.
3. Ibid.
4. Ibid.
5. Ibid.
6. Ibid., 53.
7. Ibid., 52.
8. Ibid., 53.
9. Ibid., 59.
10. Ibid., 61.

CHAPTER 4

1. Bernstein, 83.
2. Ibid., 78.
3. Ibid., 80.
4. Ibid., 86.
5. Ibid.
6. Ibid., 87.
7. Ibid.
8. Ibid., 90.
9. Ibid., 91.

10. Ibid., 92.
11. Timothy Dwight, *Travels in New-England and New-York,* Volume 4. New Haven, Conn.: S. Converse, 1822, 124.
12. Bernstein, 94.
13. Ibid., 101.

CHAPTER 5

1. Bernstein, 102.
2. Ibid.
3. Carol Sheriff, *The Artificial River: The Erie Canal and the Paradox of Progress, 1817–1862.* New York: Hill and Wang, 1996, 18.
4. Bernstein, 106.
5. Sheriff, 18.
6. Bernstein, 109.
7. Ibid.
8. Ibid., 110.
9. Ibid., 118.
10. Ibid., 121.
11. Ibid., 122.
12. Ibid., 109.
13. Ibid., 125.
14. Ibid.

CHAPTER 6

1. John Lambert, *Travels Through Canada and the United States in the Years 1806, 1807, 1808,* Volume 2. London: Baldwin, Craddock, and Joy, 1810, 54, 64.
2. Bernstein, 137.
3. Ibid., 148.

4. Ibid., 151.

5. Dorothie Bobe, *DeWitt Clinton.* New York: Minton, Balch, 1933, 210–211.

6. Ronald E. Shaw, *Erie Water West: A History of the Erie Canal, 1792–1854.* Lexington: University of Kentucky Press, 1966, 48.

7. Ibid., 50.

8. Ibid., 53.

9. Ibid., 55.

CHAPTER 7

1. Shaw, 56.

2. Ibid., 69.

3. Ibid., 88.

4. Bernstein, 204.

5. Shaw, 97.

6. Ibid., 99.

CHAPTER 8

1. Shaw, 99.

2. Bernstein, 262.

3. Shaw, 125.

4. Bernstein, 267.

5. Ibid., 270.

6. Ibid.

7. Ibid., 272.

8. Ibid., 263.

9. Ibid., 265.

10. Ibid.

CHAPTER 9

1. Bernstein, 281.

2. Sheriff, 45.

3. Ibid., 58.

4. Ibid., 59.

CHAPTER 10

1. Bernstein, 312.

BIBLIOGRAPHY

Bernstein, Peter L. *Wedding of the Waters: The Erie Canal and the Making of a Great Nation.* New York: W.W. Norton, 2005.

Bobe, Dorothie. *DeWitt Clinton.* New York: Minton, Balch, 1933.

Buehr, Walter. *Through the Locks: Canals Today and Yesterday.* New York: G.P. Putnam's Sons, 1954.

Dwight, Timothy. *Travels in New England and New York,* Volume 4. New Haven, Conn.: S. Converse, 1822.

Hecht, Roger W., ed. *The Erie Canal Reader: 1790–1950.* Syracuse, N.Y.: Syracuse University Press, 2003.

Lambert, John. *Travels Through Canada and the United States in the Years 1806, 1807, 1808,* Volume 2. London: Baldwin, Craddock, and Joy, 1810.

Levy, Janey. *The Erie Canal: A Primary Source History of the Canal That Changed America.* New York: Rosen Publishing Company, 2003.

Martin, James Kirby, et al. *America and Its People.* New York: HarperCollins, 1993.

Shaw, Ronald E. *Erie Water West: A History of the Erie Canal, 1792–1854.* Lexington: University of Kentucky Press, 1966.

Sheriff, Carol. *The Artificial River: The Erie Canal and the Paradox of Progress, 1817–1862.* New York: Hill and Wang, 1996.

FURTHER READING

Doherty, Craig A., and Katherine M. Doherty. *The Erie Canal.* Woodbridge, Conn.: Blackbirch, 1997.

Larkin, F. Daniel. *New York State Canals: A Short History.* Fleischmanns, N.Y.: Purple Mountain Press, 1998.

————, Julie C. Daniels, and Jean West, eds. *Erie Canal: New York's Gift to the Nation, A Document-Based Teacher Resource.* Peterborough, N.H.: Cobblestone Publishing, 2001.

McFee, Michele A. *A Long Haul: The Story of the New York State Barge Canal.* Fleischmanns, N.Y.: Purple Mountain Press, 1998.

Nirgiotis, Nicholas. *Erie Canal: Gateway to the West.* New York: Franklin Watts, 1993.

Sandak, Cass R. *Canals.* New York: Franklin Watts, 1983.

Spangenburg, Ray, and Diane Moser. *The Story of America's Canals.* New York: Facts on File, 1992.

Spier, Peter. *The Erie Canal.* New York: Doubleday, 1990.

Stone, Tanya Lee. *America's Top 10 Construction Wonders.* Woodbridge, Conn.: Blackbirch Press, 1998.

WEB SITES

The Erie Canal
http://www.eriecanal.org/

The Erie Canal Reader, 1790–1950
http://www.syracuseuniversitypress.syr.edu/spring-2003-catalog/erie-canal.html

New York State Erie Canal Tourism

http://www.nycanal.com/

New York State: NYS Canals

http://www.canals.state.ny.us/

University of Rochester Department of History: History of the Erie Canal

http://www.history.rochester.edu/canal/

Photo Credits

INDEX

ABOUT THE AUTHOR

TIM McNEESE is associate professor of history at York College in York, Nebraska, where he is in his seventeenth year of college instruction. Professor McNeese earned an associate of arts degree from York College, a bachelor of arts in history and political science from Harding University, and a master of arts in history from Missouri State University. A prolific writer of books for elementary, middle, high school, and college readers, McNeese has published more than 100 books and educational materials over the past 20 years, on everything from the founding of New York to Hispanic authors. His writing has earned him a citation in the library reference work *Contemporary Authors* and multiple citations in *Best Books for Young Teen Readers*. In 2006, Tim appeared on the History Channel program, *Risk Takers, History Makers: John Wesley Powell and the Grand Canyon.* He was a faculty member at the 2006 Tony Hillerman Writers Conference in Albuquerque. His wife, Beverly, is an assistant professor of English at York College. They have two married children, Noah and Summer, and three grandchildren, Ethan, Adrianna, and Finn William. Tim and Bev sponsored study trips for college students on the Lewis and Clark Trail in 2003 and 2005 and to the American Southwest in 2008. You may contact Professor McNeese at tdmcneese@york.edu.